UNDERSTANDING WORSHIP

A *PRAXIS* STUDY GUIDE

Mark Earey, Perran Gay
and Anne Horton

MOWBRAY
London and New York

MOWBRAY

A Continuum imprint

The Tower Building
11 York Road
London
SE1 7NX

First published 2001

British Library Cataloguing-in-Publication Data
A catalogue record for this book is available from the British Library

ISBN 0-264-67505-3

Printed and bound in Great Britain by Martins the Printers

CONTENTS

INTRODUCTION

THE three authors of this book are committed to promoting a deeper understanding of worship and encouraging good practice. We have worked for this through our longstanding involvement with *Praxis*, as members of its Council. Since its formation in 1990, *Praxis* has always taken a practical approach to worship education and liturgical formation. One of its aims is 'to serve congregations and clergy in their exploration of the call to worship'. The vision behind this book was to fulfil that aim by providing some teaching resources that could be useful in a variety of contexts, from parish home groups, study groups, or Lent courses, to training courses for lay or ordained ministries. You won't find a full-scale course in liturgy here, but there should be enough to give you a good start.

The three authors all have hands-on experience of leading worship and of adult education, and come from differing traditions within the Church of England. The writing of the book has been a genuinely collaborative effort. Though each session was originally drafted by one of us, in each case the writing was preceded by conversation about the shape and content of that session. After an initial draft, each part has been worked over by the three of us, individually and in face to face conversation. Each of us is glad to own the whole book, and we hope that it will be useful to the whole Church. We have not shied away from contentious issues when they have been raised, but we have tried to avoid taking party lines, believing fully in the second of the aims of *Praxis*, that it should 'provide a forum in which different worshipping traditions can meet and interact'. Hence we have found the whole process both fulfilling and challenging. We hope that this will also be the case for those who use the material.

to serve congregations and clergy in their exploration of the call to worship

As well as theological and liturgical emphases, people differ in how much they like to be told, how much they like to discuss, how much history and background they prefer and how much practical content they want that relates to their own experience. We have tried to provide a balance over the sessions of the course. Some will no doubt enjoy some sessions or some parts of sessions more than others, but we hope that there is something here for everyone. Because of the different users in mind, no one is likely to find the

to provide a forum in which different worshipping traditions can meet and interact material usable straight from the book. For some it will be too detailed, for some not detailed enough. We have tried to ensure that there is a good amount of input in each session, simply because we sense that there are a lot of worshippers who are asking basic (and not so basic) questions about 'why we do . . .' in our services. On

to enrich the practice and understanding of worship in the Church of England

the whole there is probably more discussion material and input than most people will want to use. We hope that different users will feel free to supplement, omit and alter these resources as suits their own situations.

We have thoroughly enjoyed working together in writing this book. Each of us has benefited from the skills and knowledge of the others. Our prayer is that others will gain as much joy in using it, and that in the process the third of the aims of *Praxis* will be fulfilled: 'to enrich the practice and understanding of worship in the Church of England'. *Praxis* was set up in the belief that worship is 'a primary expression of the Christian faith'. We firmly believe that deeper understanding leads to richer involvement in the liturgy, which in turn results in people becoming more open to the transforming power of God as they engage with him in worship and serve him in the world.

Mark Earey, Perran Gay and Anne Horton

"a primary expression of the Christian faith"

USING THIS BOOK

The group leader

Understanding Worship has been written for group leaders and aims to equip them with the basic information they need to lead the various sessions. The material assumes a small local church study group and a group leader. The group leader does not have to be a worship expert. Anyone who regularly attends Church of England worship, and is appreciative of and familiar with its services, already has sufficient knowledge for leading group discussion. Basic background information is given in the text. For those who want to read a little more deeply into the subject matter of each session, there are supplementary reading and resource suggestions.

Session content and structure

The book is ordered so that each session moves from the wider context of worship into the details of particular services. While the best use of the book would be to use all the sessions in order, it would be perfectly possible, for example, to run the course as three sets of four sessions instead of a straight run of twelve or, indeed, to select just four or six sessions and either run a short course or spread the material across a larger number of meetings. The book layout is aimed to assist course planning. For each session there is a session plan, pages of input information and photocopiable pages of handouts and visuals.

Each session has a common structure:

Part A – Getting Started
❖ Practical 'Leader's Preparation' notes
❖ Opening worship ideas
❖ A 'Session Starter' idea

Part B – Heart of the Matter
❖ Input and background material, which incorporates suggestions for discussion. The visuals and handouts support this material.

Part C – Taking it Further
❖ An idea or two for further discussion if there is time
❖ Ideas for closing worship
❖ A list of 'Reading and Resource' materials
❖ A simple task to be completed by group members before the next session.

Group leaders will need to plan exactly how long to spend on each part of the sessions. As a rough guide, we suggest you allow about 15 minutes in all for worship, about 15 minutes for the session starter and about 70 minutes for all the input and discussion. Feel free to be flexible, according to the needs of your group; and, indeed, to be selective, particularly over your choice of discussion questions.

Worship

Suggestions are made for opening and closing worship. These are not intended to be restrictive; leaders may wish to introduce appropriate variations. It is good to have some focus for the worship. This may be quite simple: a small table on which a cross or icon and a candle can be placed. In the different sessions, you may like to incorporate other appropriate articles, such as a Bible. You may like to cover the table with appropriate coloured drapes. The group leader does not always have to lead the worship; this is something you may like to ask a group member to do. Sometimes the singing (or reading aloud) of hymns or songs is suggested. Tapes and CDs are a helpful substitute for live accompaniment.

WORKING WITH THE GROUP

Group members will have their own experience and knowledge and are important learning resources for each other. Group leaders with some knowledge of the members of the group will be better able to help each individual to listen to and learn from the others. Listening to and affirming everybody's contribution encourages every group member, however timid, to participate. Worship is a subject that can engender strong emotions. It is important to chair the discussion so that no one member, however knowledgeable, dominates at the expense of the contributions of others. A good group leader will also need to be sensitive to differing views according to people's various church backgrounds. Each person's distinctive ideas can make a valuable contribution to everyone's learning.

Clear 'ground rules' are helpful and confidentiality must be respected. It is also important to be clear about time commitment. Group members will appreciate knowing how long each session will take, and that they will begin and end on time. An appropriate length of time for each session might be two hours, including a short break for refreshments.

Hospitality

Groups function best in congenial surroundings! The group leader should make sure that the venue for the meetings is booked and published. Comfortable chairs, arranged in the round, are recommended. Round table discussions are more inhibiting. Most groups will appreciate a refreshment break. Often an existing group will have developed its own routine, but, if not, the leader needs to plan in a break time, and to ask someone, not necessarily the host, to make the necessary provision. It is difficult both to lead the group and to look after the refreshments.

Preparing for each session

As you prepare each session make a note of the resources you will need. Handout material for photocopying is incorporated in the text, as are some suggested 'visuals'. There may be other material you need to make available. Ask people to bring paper and something with which to write. It helps if group members bring their own Bibles and Service books to the sessions. If not, have a supply on hand for people to use (or copies of the service material they need for reference.) Large sheets of paper and coloured pens are always useful. Flip chart pads are obtainable from most stationers. The visuals were designed with overhead projection in mind. (Visuals are generally printed four to a page; they can be enlarged to A4 size and photocopied on to acetates.) However, the visuals page could, alternatively, be photocopied as it is and used as a second handout. Some session notes suggest that music might be played; make sure that the appropriate equipment is set up and working before the session starts.

THE STORY OF CHRISTIAN WORSHIP: FOUNDATIONS

PART A – GETTING STARTED

Aim

To give an historical overview of Christian worship, laying the foundations for later sessions and giving an opportunity for participants to explore their own assumptions about worship.

Leader's preparation

Sessions 1 and 2 provide the historical framework for all that follows. Depending on the level of existing knowledge in the group, you may feel it is appropriate to photocopy some or all of the 'Heart of the Matter' sections as an additional handout.

Depending on how you structure the session and how well the group members already know each other you will probably find that there is too much discussion material. Be selective and, if necessary, be ready to stretch these sessions across more than two meetings of the group.

Unlike most of the other sessions, this one has two handouts, rather than a handout and four visuals. Make sure that you have enough copies for everyone.

Opening worship

Use the prayer printed on the handout ('God be in my head . . .') as a preparation for this session and for the whole course. You could read it slowly, leaving long pauses between each line. If the group have copies of the words, you could then invite them to say it together.

If possible have some visual focus, such as a lighted candle, an open Bible, or an icon or other picture. It may be helpful to use the same elements as part of the 'default' setting of the room for the worship each time the group meets, to give a sense of continuity and to help people to associate these things with a time of worship.

Session starter

If this is the first meeting of the group (rather than an already existing group) you will need to spend some time introducing yourselves to one another. The following suggestions could be part of that, allowing people to talk to one another in pairs:

❖ Think back over the time you have been a Christian and about the way that worship has changed (either in the church you belong to, or from your experience of worshipping in different churches). Which of the changes has felt most significant for you?

❖ If the group includes those who have only recently become Christians, ask them to reflect instead on what aspects of worship made the biggest impression on them when they first started coming to church – perhaps because they found them difficult, challenging, intriguing, confusing, inspiring, etc.

Other session starters might include working in pairs on one of the following (particularly appropriate if members of the group already know each other well):

❖ Use section 1 on handout 1 ('What inspires you?') and invite people to share their answers in pairs or groups of three.

❖ In pairs or groups of three use the grid at section 2 of handout 1 ('What is worship?') to think about the definition of worship. Be ready to share your thoughts briefly with the rest of the group.

PART B – HEART OF THE MATTER

See pages 10–13

PART C – TAKING IT FURTHER

For further discussion

Are there any aspects of worship in your church about which people would say things like, 'We've *always* done it this way'? Do these need investigating?

Reading and resources

Some of these resources will be useful across the whole course, and not just for this first session:

James F. White, *Introduction to Christian Worship* (Abingdon Press, revised edn. 1990) – a useful, concise introduction to the history of Christian worship.

Evelyn Underhill, *Worship* (Nisbet, 1936 and many reprints) – a classic, full of wisdom and still very useful.

Kenneth Stevenson, *The First Rites: Worship in the Early Church* (Lamp/Marshall Pickering, 1989) – a brief introduction to the early history of all major services from Holy Communion to Funerals.

Geoffrey Cuming, *A History of Anglican Liturgy* (Macmillan, 2nd edn. 1982) – for those who want the nitty gritty of Anglican liturgical history.

Stephen Dean, ed., *Celebration: The Liturgy Handbook* (Geoffrey Chapman, 1993) – an accessible study book for lay people, based on the Roman Catholic Syllabus of Liturgical Formation, *Celebrating the Paschal Mystery*. Good 'comparison' reading for those who act as group leaders for *Understanding Worship*.

Closing worship

Have two people ready to read Amos 5.21–24 and Romans 12.1–2. Read the first, keep a time of silence and then read the second.

Consider singing one of the following or some other song or hymn (or, try to find a recording to which you could listen):

❖ For all the saints – W. Walsham How;

❖ We have a gospel to proclaim – Edward Burns;

❖ When the music fades ('The heart of worship') – Matt Redman.

Before the next session

Try to write your own one-sentence explanation of what 'worship' is. Imagine you are writing for a friend who has no church or religious background, and who has been wondering what on earth people think they are doing when they go to church.

PART B – HEART OF THE MATTER

BACK TO SQUARE ONE: WORSHIP IN THE NEW TESTAMENT

It would be very convenient if Jesus or Saint Paul had left us with instructions about what should happen in a service at church. They didn't – though often people in the church (of all backgrounds and traditions) have acted as if they did. The New Testament contains clues, but no more, to the worship of the first Christians.

 DISCUSSION

Where would you look in the New Testament for guidance about worship? Possible places to start might include:

❖ Acts 2.43–47. Note that the emphasis is on the believers being together. Although there is an outline of what was included, here, as elsewhere in Acts, we have no detail of exactly what they did or how they did it.

❖ Passages in Revelation about the worship of heaven.

❖ Paul's partial account of the Lord's Supper in 1 Corinthians 11 and his instructions about the use of tongues in 1 Corinthians 14.

❖ Colossians 3.16–17 '... sing psalms, hymns and spiritual songs ... do everything in the name of the Lord Jesus, giving thanks to God the Father through him.'

There are also many passages that may have originally been used in the worship of the first Christians. Examples include Luke 1.46-54 (Mary's song), Luke 1.68–79 (Zechariah's song), Luke 2. 29–32 (Simeon's song), Philippians 2.6-11 and 1 Timothy 3.16. In modern Bible versions they are easier to spot because they are set out like poetry. We have no proof (a poetic form does not necessarily mean that this was a hymn or piece of spoken worship), but we can guess.

Jewish roots

The first Christians were Jews and brought some of their Jewish assumptions about worship over into the new 'sect'. We do not have very clear information about Jewish worship at the time of Jesus (most of our sources date from after the first century), but in general terms it seems that there were three focuses of worship:

❖ The temple – a place of sacrifice, of prayer, of music and singing, of learning (see for example the boy Jesus in Luke 2.41–52). Worship was formal, ordered and led by hereditary priests and trained musicians.

❖ The synagogue – a place of the word and prayer. Led by authorized lay persons, the services were less formally structured and focused on reading from the scriptures, preaching and prayer. See Luke 4.14-22.

❖ The home – where the basics of the faith were passed on, stories shared and prayer offered. Every meal was an opportunity to give thanks to God – a pattern that Christians have inherited in the practice of saying grace at meals.

At first the followers of Jesus joined in worship with other Jews. They attended the temple for prayer and participated in the synagogues, though it seems that they supplemented this with worship on their own, mainly in homes. However, Christians also began to see that key elements of Jewish worship (such as the temple, the priesthood and sacrifice) had been fulfilled in Jesus and continued to be fulfilled in his followers:

❖ The **temple** – Christians saw Christ as one in whom God 'dwelt' and through whom God dwelt among his people (John 1.14 and Colossians 1.19). As those who were 'in Christ', believers saw themselves also as the new temple of God both individually and corporately (1 Corinthians 3.16–17; 6.19 and 14.25).

❖ The **priesthood** – Jesus is the great high priest (Hebrews 9.11–14), with no further need for human intermediaries. Christians saw themselves corporately as a royal priesthood: bringing the world to God in prayer and presenting the message of God's salvation to the world.

❖ The **sacrifices** – fulfilled in Jesus himself (through his self-sacrifice on the cross) and in the lives of his people, offering praise and living for God in the world (Hebrews 9.12-14; 13.12-16 and Romans 12.1)

 DISCUSSION

❖ In what different contexts do you worship? At home? At church? At work, college or school? In a small group (such as a home group, youth group, Mothers' Union group etc.)?

❖ What are the practical problems you face in terms of worship in the home, either as an individual or with other members of the household? Can you think of any solutions?

THE EARLY CHURCH IN THE ROMAN WORLD

In AD 70 the temple in Jerusalem was destroyed by the Romans. Many Christians, along with Jews, were expelled from the city. Jewish worship could no longer be focused on the temple and so the synagogue and domestic worship grew in importance. It also brought greater contact between the new 'Way' and the non-Jewish world, all of which influenced the development of Christian worship.

We tend to think of the first Christians hiding in the catacombs and conducting their worship in secret, and in part this is true. The persecution of Christians, however, was neither constant nor uniform around the Roman world.

On the whole, Christian worship developed in a domestic setting. In towns, wealthier Christians opened their large homes (usually built around an open courtyard) to the local believers for worship on 'the Lord's day' (Sunday). This provided a discreet way for Christians to join together in worship in groups that were larger than families but not huge.

Where there was no suitable home, or where numbers were larger or persecution fiercer, it seems that Christians met outside the towns in the open. Sunday was a working day and so the believers met early, before work began. There was no one original form of service or way of worship. The early Church included great diversity, and it was only in later centuries that these diverse forms begin to converge around particular 'families' of rites with common features and common words.

A major turning point

A major change for Christian worship began in AD 312. This was the year that the Roman emperor, Constantine, was victorious at the battle of the Milvian Bridge. Ascribing the victory to the God of the Christians, he became a Christian himself – and, unsurprisingly, brought most of the empire with him.

Though Christianity did not become the official state religion until AD 380, the Christian Church changed rapidly from being a sporadically persecuted minority religion to being the religion of choice for those who wanted to 'get on' in the empire. Christian leaders became significant figures in the world and Christian worship went from being primarily a small-scale and 'domestic' affair, to being a large-scale, formal, public event. It was at this stage that many of the things we take for granted were introduced:

❖ Large church buildings were built, modelled not on religious temples, but on the basilica, a civic building like a town hall.

❖ The 'style' of worship began to be modelled on Roman civic life. This meant processions, 'vestments', and ceremonial all became more prominent in worship.

❖ Local patterns of worship begin to conform to prestigious centres (such as Rome, Constantinople and Milan). The growing popularity of pilgrimage meant that people were more aware of what was happening in other places, and pilgrims brought back ideas which were put into practice back at home.

❖ In time, Sunday became a public holiday.

❖ A concern for orthodoxy led to the fixing of the words used in worship and the decline of spontaneity and extemporary prayer.

 DISCUSSION

Many aspects of Christian and Church of England worship in this country derive from close connections with the state. For instance:

❖ the restrictions on shopping and other activities on a Sunday (even though many of these restrictions have now been eased, Sunday is still not treated as the same as every other day);

❖ the use of parish churches and cathedrals for 'civic' services;

❖ the rights of those who live in a parish to marry in the parish church, to have their children baptized there, and to be buried in the churchyard (if there is one) when they die;

❖ the place of Church of England bishops in the upper house of Parliament.

Group members may be able to think of other examples. Discuss the pros and cons of this connection as it relates to worship. What parallels can you see with the church's situation in the fourth century?

East and West

The division of the Roman Empire into East and West in the fourth century was paralleled in the Church. Worship in the West began to settle into families of rites, which were eventually dominated by the pattern of Rome. Worship in the East followed Antioch, Alexandria and Jerusalem, and eventually tended to follow Constantinople. The Western pattern of worship evolved and changed: the Eastern tended to stabilize around one or two particular forms – the Liturgy of St John Chrysostom being the most commonly used. This stability is still the pattern today in the Eastern (or 'Orthodox') traditions.

Worship in England

When Augustine arrived from Rome in 597 with the Christian gospel, the Celtic Church had already been active in parts of Britain for some time. The two traditions clashed and, at the Synod of Whitby in 664, decisions were taken that would affect the worship of God in this country for centuries. The Roman pattern was to dominate in England as elsewhere in the West. One of the consequences was the development of the parish system. The country was divided into settled worshipping communities each with a parish priest, rather than being served by itinerant ministers, as was the Celtic pattern.

By the medieval period, worship had become clergy dominated and the people participated mainly by attending, watching and listening, and possibly getting on with their own devotions, rather than by active and vocal participation in the words and actions of the services.

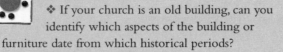

DISCUSSION

❖ If your church is an old building, can you identify which aspects of the building or furniture date from which historical periods?

❖ Have there been significant changes in your church building or its furniture or decoration in the last forty years or so? If so, what understandings of God and of worship have been reflected in these changes?

Reform and renewal

Though the break with the authority of Rome came in the lifetime of Henry VIII (1490–1547), it was during the short reign of his son, Edward VI (1547–1553), that the principles of the Reformation began to affect the worship of the Church in England in a major way. An English translation of the Bible had been set up in every parish church and the Lord's Prayer, Creed and Ten Commandments were to be said in English. However, the major changes to the orders of service were to take place later under the guiding hand (and pen) of the Archbishop of Canterbury, Thomas Cranmer (1489–1556).

1548

A penitential section in English was added to the end of the Latin Mass and, for the first time for centuries, the people were offered Communion regularly (both bread *and* wine).

1549

The first full prayer book in English was published. There were many changes in the words to suit the new doctrines of the Reformation, but the 'look and feel' (vestments, candles, ceremonial etc.) of the services was little changed.

1552

Another new Prayer Book was published. This was a more thoroughgoing revision which applied Reformed principles to the instructions as well as the words of the services. This was accompanied by more obvious changes to other aspects of the worship: for instance, vestments were forbidden in favour of the simple surplice, and altars were destroyed and replaced by moveable tables.

Cranmer's aim in all his work was that the worship should be:

❖ Understandable by the people;

❖ Simple in form, to avoid obscurity and superstitious understanding;

❖ Biblical in content.

The sixteenth-century Reformation followed hot on the heels of the invention of printing and the printed book was to become a key feature in the Church of England's understanding of worship. Without the invention of printing it would have been impossible for Cranmer to have imposed a new service book uniformly on the whole Church in England quickly, at the same time, and at a fixed price (to ensure that no churchwardens could resist on the basis of cost). The liturgy in English, greatly simplified and exactly the same in every parish church, gave the *The Book of Common Prayer* a very special role in the Church of England. It became not only a liturgical manual in the hands of the priest (as the old books had been) but also a doctrinal standard, and later a devotional book, known by heart and often owned and kept at home as well as available in the parish church. Because the liturgy was accessible to the laity it gave the laity, for the first time, the ability to 'check up' on the priest: the laity were liturgically empowered. The folk memory of this, and its association with the printed book, dies hard. There is still a suspicion in the mind of some Church of England worshippers that a fast one is being pulled if what they are offered by way of an order of service is not the same as the book in the hands of the priest.

DISCUSSION

❖ What are the technological changes this century that rival the importance of the invention of printing in the fifteenth century (and its impact in the sixteenth century)?

❖ Can you see any ways in which these technological changes are influencing contemporary assumptions about worship in ways that parallel the influence of printing over Anglican assumptions about worship and books?

Change and change again

However, history was against Cranmer. He was burnt at the stake in 1556 and the reign of Queen Mary returned England to Roman Catholic forms of worship. The accession of Elizabeth in 1558 brought an element of compromise – a Protestant religion, but not as thoroughly Reformed as Cranmer might have liked. Cranmer's 1552 Prayer Book was re-imposed, with some minor changes. However, even this was not to last. During the period of the Commonwealth in the seventeenth century the use of the Prayer Book was abolished altogether. It was replaced in 1645 with *The Directory for the Public Worship of God* – a guide for clergy about how to devise services, with no fixed forms of liturgy prescribed.

It was the restoration of the monarchy after the Commonwealth period that gave us *The Book of Common Prayer* of 1662

(BCP), so familiar to generations of worshippers in the Church of England. The 1662 Prayer Book was basically Cranmer's 1552 text, but with some small changes, not least to the rubrics and instructions, to suit the breadth of opinion by then existing in the Church of England.

DISCUSSION

If you were reforming the Church of England (or even your own local church) what would be your key principles?

Liturgy and life

In the Church of England we tend to use the word 'liturgy' when talking about worship. 'Liturgy' is a Greek word rooted in the early history of Christian worship, and means something like, 'the work (or offering) of the people', or, 'public works'. It occurs often in the New Testament, often translated as 'ministry' or 'service'. It is used to refer to mission (Romans 15.16) and alms for the poor (Romans 15.27). It is used of corporate worship in Acts 13.2, where it seems to mean prayer. There is something inherently corporate and public about it. Though today it is sometimes used as a technical term to refer to the words of the service (as in, 'I loved the hymns this morning but I didn't like the liturgy') it is much more than that. 'Liturgy' is shorthand for a way of approaching worship which is basically structured, participatory, ritual (in the sense of including repeated or familiar actions as well as words) and symbolic.

The term 'worship' can cover a much larger field: in Christian terms our whole lives are acts of worship; offerings to God (Romans 12:1). But worship can also refer to something very private and individual; our own private prayers and devotions. Liturgy falls somewhere in between. It is bigger than our private prayers, and therefore subject to different constraints. It must take account of other people and their needs and preferences. It must be *corporate* worship, and not simply collective worship (the sum of individual devotions offered by people who happen to be in the same room). Yet it is also smaller than 'worship'. Liturgy, by definition, takes place when we meet with God's people specifically in order to worship God. Though it relates to the rest of our lives, it must do so primarily symbolically, energizing and enthusing, calling us to live in certain ways the rest of the week. For instance, in our intercessions we can symbolically engage with God's world, sharing in Christ's priestly intercession for it, but our main engagement is to live in that world. Again, in church we read the Scriptures, but this is not merely a practical way of getting us to hear them: it symbolizes and forms in us a basic attitude to Scripture that must be lived out to be effective.

DISCUSSION

❖ Do you agree that there is a difference between 'collective' worship and 'corporate' worship? How would you describe that difference to someone else?

❖ 'The worship begins when the liturgy is over.' Do you agree?

OPENING WORSHIP

God be in my head, and in my understanding;
God be in my eyes, and in my looking;
God be in my mouth, and in my speaking;
God be in my heart, and in my thinking;
God be at my end, and at my departing.

From the Sarum Primer

1 What inspires you?

What is your favourite part of a church service?

_____

What makes it so special for you? Tick any that apply:

☐ The beauty or power of the words?

☐ The beauty or power of the music?

☐ The beauty or power of something physical
  or symbolic?

☐ The memories or associations you have with
  that part of the service?

☐ That it makes you feel specially close to God?

Something else, not mentioned above: . . . .

_____

Before the next session
Try to write your own one-sentence explanation of
what 'worship' is. Imagine you are writing for a friend
who has no church or religious background, and who
has been wondering what on earth people think they are
doing when they go to church.

2 What is worship?
Look at these definitions of worship. What would you say are
the strengths and weaknesses of each?

A

'To worship is to quicken the conscience by the holiness
of God, to feed the mind with the truth of God, to purge
the imagination by the beauty of God, to open the heart
to the love of God, to devote the will to the purpose of
God.'

William Temple

Strengths . . .   Weaknesses . . .
_____   _____

_____   _____

B

'At heart, worship is a statement of faith. We worship
because we believe in a certain kind of God.'
'Let the people worship' – Methodist report 1988

Strengths . . .   Weaknesses . . .
_____   _____

_____   _____

C

'Worship is God's enjoyment of us and our enjoyment of
him.'

Graham Kendrick ('Worship' 1984)

Strengths . . .   Weaknesses . . .
_____   _____

_____   _____

THE STORY OF CHRISTIAN WORSHIP: FOUNDATIONS

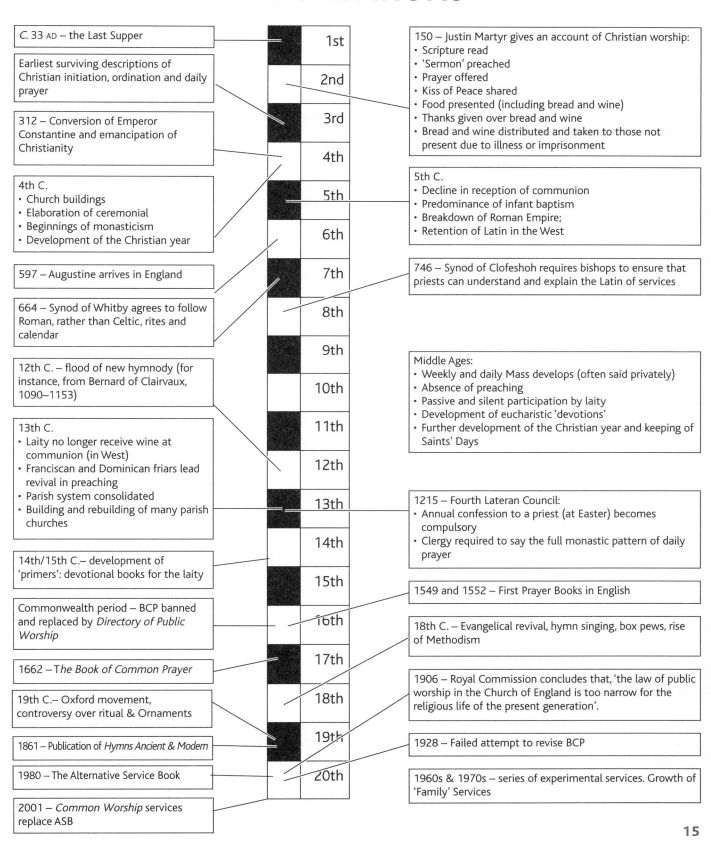

C. 33 AD – the Last Supper

Earliest surviving descriptions of Christian initiation, ordination and daily prayer

312 – Conversion of Emperor Constantine and emancipation of Christianity

4th C.
• Church buildings
• Elaboration of ceremonial
• Beginnings of monasticism
• Development of the Christian year

597 – Augustine arrives in England

664 – Synod of Whitby agrees to follow Roman, rather than Celtic, rites and calendar

12th C. – flood of new hymnody (for instance, from Bernard of Clairvaux, 1090–1153)

13th C.
• Laity no longer receive wine at communion (in West)
• Franciscan and Dominican friars lead revival in preaching
• Parish system consolidated
• Building and rebuilding of many parish churches

14th/15th C.– development of 'primers': devotional books for the laity

Commonwealth period – BCP banned and replaced by *Directory of Public Worship*

1662 – T*he Book of Common Prayer*

19th C.– Oxford movement, controversy over ritual & Ornaments

1861 – Publication of *Hymns Ancient & Modern*

1980 – The Alternative Service Book

2001 – *Common Worship* services replace ASB

1st
2nd
3rd
4th
5th
6th
7th
8th
9th
10th
11th
12th
13th
14th
15th
16th
17th
18th
19th
20th

150 – Justin Martyr gives an account of Christian worship:
• Scripture read
• 'Sermon' preached
• Prayer offered
• Kiss of Peace shared
• Food presented (including bread and wine)
• Thanks given over bread and wine
• Bread and wine distributed and taken to those not present due to illness or imprisonment

5th C.
• Decline in reception of communion
• Predominance of infant baptism
• Breakdown of Roman Empire;
• Retention of Latin in the West

746 – Synod of Clofeshoh requires bishops to ensure that priests can understand and explain the Latin of services

Middle Ages:
• Weekly and daily Mass develops (often said privately)
• Absence of preaching
• Passive and silent participation by laity
• Development of eucharistic 'devotions'
• Further development of the Christian year and keeping of Saints' Days

1215 – Fourth Lateran Council:
• Annual confession to a priest (at Easter) becomes compulsory
• Clergy required to say the full monastic pattern of daily prayer

1549 and 1552 – First Prayer Books in English

18th C. – Evangelical revival, hymn singing, box pews, rise of Methodism

1906 – Royal Commission concludes that, 'the law of public worship in the Church of England is too narrow for the religious life of the present generation'.

1928 – Failed attempt to revise BCP

1960s & 1970s – series of experimental services. Growth of 'Family' Services

THE STORY OF CHRISTIAN WORSHIP: THE LAST HUNDRED YEARS

PART A – GETTING STARTED

Aim

To consider the major changes in liturgical thinking in the last hundred years and to trace the resulting changes in the liturgy of the Church of England, including *Common Worship*.

Leader's preparation

Have a thorough look through a copy of the *Common Worship* main service book and the Pastoral Services volume, noting particularly the flexibility allowed (make sure you look at the notes at the end of each service) and the importance of structure (note the 'Structure' page that precedes each order of service).

   The time chart (Visual 3) works better on paper than projected with an OHP, and it might be wise to have this (with the two other visuals on the sheet) available as an additional handout.

Opening worship

Use *Patterns for Worship* to devise a very short act of worship which includes Praise, Action, Word, and Prayer. The elements may be shared across the opening and closing worship for this session, such that the study and discussion in the middle is seen as *part* of the act of worship itself.

Session starter

Ask members of the group to share the definitions of worship they came up with in the 'before the next session' work. Are there any things that they have in common? Does anything seem to be missing?

PART B – HEART OF THE MATTER

See pages 18–21

PART C – TAKING IT FURTHER

For further discussion

Some ecumenically and internationally agreed texts (such as the Lord's Prayer and the Nicene Creed) were rejected or amended by the Liturgical Commission or the General Synod in the process of producing and authorizing the *Common Worship* services. Which do you think is more important:

❖ to use texts that are as 'right' as we think we can make them, or

❖ to try (for the sake of unity) to agree to use the same texts as other Christians, even if we think they may not be the best version?

Reading and resources

Mark Earey and Gilly Myers (eds), *Common Worship Today* (HarperCollins, 2001) – an accessible and highly visual introduction to worship in general and to the contents of *Common Worship* in particular.

Paul Bradshaw (ed.), *Companion to Common Worship*, Volume 1 (SPCK, 2001) – an introduction to the history of liturgy and a thorough commentary on the *Common Worship* services.

R.C.D. Jasper, *The Development of the Anglican Liturgy 1662–1980* (SPCK, 1989) – a thorough account of liturgical revision up to the ASB.

John Fenwick and Bryan Spinks, *Worship in Transition: The Twentieth Century Liturgical Movement* (T&T Clark, 1995) – an ecumenical look at the movements of thought behind the changes to the texts.

Closing worship

Use the remaining elements of the act of worship with which you began the session.

Before the next session

Look at the following list of special days. Pick the three which are the most important or significant for you.

> Christmas Day
> Your birthday
> Remembrance Sunday
> Your wedding anniversary
> Mothering Sunday
> Father's Day
> Easter Day
> Other

1) How do you **prepare** for these special days?

2) How do you **celebrate** these special days?

3) What are your favourite two days in the Church's worship? (There may be overlap with the above list.)

Praise

Action

Word

PRAYER

PART B – HEART OF THE MATTER

A CENTURY OF CHANGE

As the twentieth century opened, the Church of England's worship appeared, on the surface, to be exactly as it had been since 1662.

However, though the printed words of the services were the same, at parish level there was always variation in practice from church to church and from decade to decade:

❖ From the eighteenth century, hymns increasingly brought variety to services and, you could argue, made more of a difference to the average worshipper than the text of the liturgy;

❖ Churches with differing theological emphases followed the same texts, but they interpreted and used them in very different ways, varying the way the services were led, the actions and ritual associated with them, and even the names given to the services (for example Holy Communion, Parish Mass, or Eucharist);

❖ Extra provision developed for things not in *The Book of Common Prayer* (for example, Harvest Festival and Christmas Carol Services).

NATURAL EVOLUTION

When the text of the liturgy was fixed – as it was, by law, in the Church of England – variety in worship broke out in other ways. The question was, how to respond to this variety: to attempt to crush it, to turn a blind eye, or to try to control it?

The issue was brought to a head in the latter part of the nineteenth century. The Oxford Movement and Anglo-Catholic revival had highlighted some dissatisfaction with *The Book of Common Prayer*. Some churches began making alterations to the services, using the same words but changing the order of some elements and adding a good deal of ceremonial and ritual which had previously been assumed to be illegal in the Church of England. The subsequent court cases and division within the Church led to the appointment of a Royal Commission, which reported in 1906 that 'the law of public worship in the Church of England is too narrow for the religious life of the present generation'.

DISCUSSION

❖ Do you agree that the natural state is for worship to change and vary gradually, by gentle evolution?

❖ Are there situations in which such evolution should be halted or redirected, and what are the criteria on which such decisions should be taken and who should take them?

FIRST ATTEMPTS AT CHANGE

[IT WILL BE USEFUL FOR PEOPLE TO HAVE THE TIME CHART, VISUAL 3, IN FRONT OF THEM AT VARIOUS STAGES THROUGH THIS SESSION]

The first major attempt to change or supplement *The Book of Common Prayer* culminated in a new version of the Prayer Book, which included some changes and some new options. This was rejected by Parliament in 1928 and is often referred to as the *1928 Prayer Book*. The rejection of the book by Parliament raised a new issue: who should decide on the appropriate forms of worship for the Church of England? In a society in which church attendance across the board was decreasing, including in the Church of England, how could it be right that the forms of worship were determined by a body largely comprised of non-worshippers? The paradoxes raised by this situation planted seeds that ultimately led to the law being changed in the 1960s and 70s to allow the Church to determine her own forms of worship without reference to Parliament. With the development of synodical government for the Church over the same period it could no longer be argued that the involvement of Parliament was the only guarantee of a voice for the laity in such decisions.

EXPERIMENTAL SERVICES

Despite the clear need for change, it wasn't until 1955 that the first Liturgical Commission was appointed.

The 1960s and 70s saw a number of experimental forms of service (Series 1, 2 and 3), each authorized only for a fixed number of years. These culminated in *The Alternative Service Book 1980* (ASB), which was itself only authorized initially for ten years, though this was later extended by another ten years. It is worth noting that it wasn't until the 1970s that the Church of England had services in modern English.

The Church of England (Worship and Doctrine) Act, which came into force in 1975, allowed the Church to make its own decisions about services which are alternative to those found in *The Book of Common Prayer*, without recourse to Parliament.

THE WIDER CONTEXT

All of this has taken place in the context of a century of enormous social changes and of many fresh movements within the Church itself:

❖ The **First World War** showed (through chaplains on the front line) that *The Book of Common Prayer* was no longer familiar or comprehensible to a large number of people.

❖ The **liturgical movement** advanced our understanding of the liturgy and its development. It focused on the structure and flow of worship, and not simply the words, and it stressed the importance of the corporate nature of worship and of active participation by the laity.

❖ The **charismatic movement** helped us to rediscover the Church as the body of Christ, where all have gifts from God for the building up of the whole body. This fed into the growing realization that the liturgy belongs to all God's people.

❖ The **missionary movement** has emphasized the importance of 'inculturation' – that is, encouraging forms of worship that make connections with the existing culture as well as with the Christian tradition. In Britain the Church has become more conscious of being a 'Church in mission' and many have sought ways of making worship more relevant to contemporary British culture (or cultures). The growth of 'family services' in the 1960s and 1970s was one sign of this. Another is the 'Alternative Worship' of the 1980s and 90s (such as the Nine O'clock Service and the Late Late Service).

❖ The **ecumenical movement** makes us more aware of what other denominations are doing and less wary of following their example. In scholarly terms there has been a search for models of worship that predate both the Reformation and the Eastern/Western divides. At the national and international levels, liturgists from different churches and countries try to produce agreed versions of common elements of worship (such as canticles, creeds and so on). There has also been convergence around the principle of 'freedom within a framework', which has resulted in more freedom for the 'liturgical' churches and more 'framework' for those with a non-liturgical tradition. At the local level, most congregations today include Christians whose roots are in other denominations and who were not brought up as Anglicans. Such people bring valuable experience of other ways of worship and different perspectives of what worship is all about. In addition, Local Ecumenical Partnership (LEP) churches have enabled the different traditions to learn from one another with first hand experience of regular worship rather than one-off 'united' services.

❖ New **technology** such as photocopiers and personal computers (not to mention software such as *Visual Liturgy*) has made a very significant impact on worship. They make it increasingly feasible for a church with a strong liturgical tradition, and a history of service books in the hands of the congregation, to introduce seasonal variety and local flexibility to worship. It is now economical for small local churches to produce their own printed orders of service. This makes it possible to make the most of seasonal material (such as *Lent, Holy Week, Easter* and *The Promise of His Glory*) for 'special services' or seasons (such as Good Friday, or Advent) and also enables congregations to make the most of the choices and options in services (such as between different confessions or Eucharistic Prayers) by printing their favoured pattern in an easy-to-follow order of service.

❖ The growth of what some have called **'post-modernism'** includes a greater willingness to 'mix and match' the past with the present, the traditional with the contemporary. This is reflected in *Common Worship* in two ways:

◆ Many texts are provided in both modern and traditional forms to allow them to be appropriately mixed within one service (for instance, using a traditional version of the Lord's Prayer in a modern-language Holy Communion service).

◆ The *Common Worship* main service book includes both contemporary and Prayer Book forms of service (for instance, Order One and Order Two Holy Communion services).

DISCUSSION
[SEE VISUAL 1]

❖ Invite the group members to think of any other influences on worship.

❖ To what extent and in what ways have the different influences affected the worship in your local church?

❖ If worship is primarily about God, then fresh understandings about worship will affect and change our understanding of God too. Can you think of ways that new thinking about worship has changed your understanding of God?

THE ALTERNATIVE SERVICE BOOK 1980 AND BEYOND

The Alternative Service Book 1980 was never intended to be permanent. Many of the principles that lay behind it were worked out more fully in the years following its authorization. Rather than simply extend its authorization for a further period, the opportunity was taken to reflect on twenty years of use, to make some improvements and to build in the flexibility and variety with which the Church had become familiar since 1980.

The new material was not only to replace the ASB; it was to broaden its scope and to include the most widely used parts of the Prayer Book. The result was *Common Worship*.

HOW ANGLICAN ASSUMPTIONS ABOUT WORSHIP HAVE CHANGED
[VISUAL 2]

BCP – Uniformity

National uniformity was the declared intention of liturgical policy in the 16th century. Seasonal variety was deliberately removed, in favour of simplicity. However, the Prayer Book was also seen as a 'local' form of worship in the sense that it was designed to be appropriate worship for England. The local flexibility built into the *Common Worship* services simply takes the principle a bit further. *Common Worship* is intended to make it easier for the Church of England's worship to 'fit' a local congregation and its mission context.

ASB – flexibility

The ASB gave scope for some flexibility:

❖ It used phrases like 'using these or other suitable words'.

❖ It included an element of choice (such as four Eucharistic Prayers and alternative forms of Intercession).

❖ It included much more material for different seasons and occasions – sentences, blessings, introductions to the Peace, etc.

❖ It envisaged persons other than the minister taking part (reading Scripture, leading intercessions etc.).

Post-ASB – flexibility and variety

As well as continuing the provision for flexibility and local choice, extra material produced since the ASB has added a huge variety of seasonal material.

The 'right' way to worship is now seen as something determined more by context than by law. The most appropriate worship for a small congregation will not necessarily be the best for a large one; urban may not require the same as rural; an evening service may need different treatment from a morning one, and so on.

DISCUSSION

Look at the two quotations at section 1 on the handout.

❖ How does the Church of England's liturgy feel to you in recent years? Too rigid, too flexible, or about right?

❖ What do you think would be on God's list of criteria for worship that would please him?

COMMONALITY AND DIVERSITY

The scope for local decision-making in *Common Worship* has implications for the concept of 'common prayer' within the Church of England. Shared forms of worship have been a major factor in the history of the Church of England and have functioned as doctrinal norms as well as providing a sense of family identity.

The Liturgical Commission first raised these issues in *The Renewal of Common Prayer* (1993, CHP/SPCK). They concluded that the way forward for Church of England worship was no longer uniformity, but a broader sense of 'family likeness'. This could be fostered by a combination of **clear structures** for services with an 'evolving core' of **familiar texts**.

The Liturgical Commission also raised the 'family identity' issue in *Patterns for Worship*:

'What are the marks of Anglican worship that we might expect to find (or have a right to find?) in any service? We believe that some of the marks which should be safeguarded for those who wish to stand in any recognizable continuity with historic Anglican tradition are:

❖ A clear structure for worship;

❖ An emphasis on reading the Word of God and on using psalms;

❖ Liturgical words repeated by the congregation, some of which, like the Creed, would be known by heart;

❖ Using a collect, the Lord's Prayer, and some responsive forms in prayer;

❖ A recognition of the centrality of the Eucharist;

❖ A concern for form, dignity, and economy of words.

Another mark of Anglican worship is a willingness to use forms and prayers which can be used across a broad spectrum of Christian belief. This may sometimes mean that, for the sake of the unity of the Church, we refrain from using some words which reflect one of the traditional "party" positions.'

Patterns for Worship, p. 5

[A SHORTER VERSION OF THIS EXTRACT IS GIVEN ON THE HANDOUT, SECTION 2.]

DISCUSSION

❖ How do you feel about the 'marks of Anglican worship' outlined in the quote from *Patterns for Worship*? Would you omit any from this list, or add any others?

❖ How important is 'commonality' in worship to you?

❖ Commonality raises the question of 'in common with whom?' Use the table at section 3 on the handout to help people think about this issue. To put it in more concrete terms, it is asking, 'Is it more important to use the same version of the Lord's Prayer as the Methodists who meet round the corner from us, or the version used by Anglicans in Kidderminster or Canada?'

❖ Can you think of other ways that we share in common worship: for instance, by the use of the same hymns or songs?

COMMON WORSHIP

The liturgical material which replaced the ASB has the generic title *Common Worship: Services and Prayers for the Church of England*. There are several features worth noting:

❖ *Common Worship* services have no 'sell by' date. Unlike the ASB they are authorized until 'further resolution of General Synod' – i.e. until it becomes obvious that it is time to think again – whether that is after ten years or one hundred.

❖ *Common Worship* is not a book. It is a collection of services and resources, being published in *several* books, as separate service booklets, on simple cards, on computer disk and on the internet.

❖ Among the *Common Worship* volumes there is a 'Sunday' volume – a sort of 'core' book that contains services likely to be needed for the main worship of a congregation, and that does not contain material such as funerals or marriage.

DISCUSSION

If you were devising a 'core' Sunday Service book, what services would you include in it

❖ if it were for your congregation?

❖ if it were for the whole Church of England?

Compare with the contents list of the main *Common Worship* volume.

PRINCIPLES BEHIND COMMON WORSHIP (HANDOUT SECTION 4)

There are some aspects of background thinking which are common to all the *Common Worship* services. One way of thinking about these aspects is to see them as reflecting the need for connections.

Importance of structure and shape

This is reflected in two ways:

❖ Each service begins with a page which sets out the basic structure of the service, giving a sense of the major sections, key elements, and the shape and flow of the service. Within the services care has been taken to use clear headings to show major sections as well as each item.

❖ Some 'outline' orders of service have been provided, such as A Service of the Word (see Session 6 for more detail), A Service of the Word with a Celebration of Holy Communion, and The Outline Order for Funerals. These orders of service provide a 'framework' with considerable flexibility about the texts used to fill in the detail.

Reflection of wider culture

There is an attempt to see worship in the context of mission (in its widest sense of 'the work God has given the Church to do'). There are several implications:

❖ The need to build in local flexibility so that worship can be suited to the community served by each congregation.

❖ The 'postmodernism' influence means that the Church is encouraged to value both new and old. *Common Worship* deliberately includes both.

❖ The use of 'inclusive language' in relation to people, recognizing that the use of English is changing. For instance, avoiding phrases that use 'men' or 'man' to mean all human beings, male and female.

❖ A richer style, including a broader range of biblical imagery and drawing on a variety of ways of addressing God.

Pastoral reality and 'staged rites'

Common Worship links public liturgy with pastoral resources (e.g. as well as a funeral service, there are also prayers at the time of death, prayers the night before a funeral, an act of remembrance on the anniversary of a death, etc.).

A staged rite is one in which the 'action' is spread over a series of liturgical 'stages' (reflecting the pastoral reality) rather than being focused in one service. This is most obvious with services such as initiation or funerals and the result is a tendency to produce not 'a service', but 'packages' of material.

There is also an attempt to forge links between private devotion and public liturgy (for instance, with the provision of A Form of Preparation, which can be used before Holy Communion services).

Connections with other Christians

Ecumenically, the importance of structure and shape in the revision and renewal of worship in the main 'liturgical' Churches means that Anglican worshippers can also find familiar elements in the worship of (for instance) Methodists or Roman Catholics.

In addition, some of the words of the *Common Worship* services have been chosen to bring us into line with forms used by other Christians.

Hence 'common prayer' (in the sense of 'family likeness') is now a concept that crosses denominational boundaries.

session 2 – HANDOUT

1 Change and stability

'It hath been the wisdom of the Church of England, ever since the first compiling of her Publick Liturgy, to keep the mean between the two extremes, of too much stiffness in refusing, and of too much easiness in admitting any variation from it.'

from the Preface to The Book
of Common Prayer, written in 1661

'… the law of public worship in the Church of England is too narrow for the religious life of the present generation.'

One of the conclusions of the Royal Commission
on Ecclesiastical Discipline, 1906

2 What does it mean to be 'Anglican'?

'What are the marks of Anglican worship that we might expect to find (or have a right to find?) in any service? We believe that some of the marks . . . are:

- A clear structure for worship;

- An emphasis on reading the word of God and on using psalms;

- Liturgical words repeated by the congregation, some of which, like the creed, would be known by heart;

- Using a collect, the Lord's Prayer, and some responsive forms in prayer;

- A recognition of the centrality of the Eucharist;

- A concern for form, dignity, and economy of words.'

Patterns for Worship, p. 5

3 Commonality and diversity

Sharing common forms of worship can be a way of symbolizing unity between Christians. But it raises the question of 'in common with whom?' Can you rank the following in order of importance (1 being the group with whom, in your view, it is most important to share common forms and words in worship, and 5 being the group with whom it matters least):

☐ Other Church of England churches?

☐ Other churches of different denominations in your locality?

☐ Other Churches of different denominations in the same country?

☐ Other Anglican churches around the world?

☐ English-speaking churches of other denominations around the world?

4 Principles behind *Common Worship*

❖ Importance of structure and shape

❖ Reflection of wider culture

❖ Pastoral reality and 'staged rites'

❖ Connections with other Christians

Before the next session

Look at this list of special days. Pick the three which are most important or significant for you.

☐ Christmas Day   ☐ Your birthday
☐ Remembrance Sunday   ☐ Your wedding
                           anniversary

☐ Mothering Sunday   ☐ Father's Day
☐ Easter Day   ☐ Other

1) How do you **prepare** for these special days?

2) How do you **celebrate** these special days?

3) What are your favourite two days in the Church's worship? (There may be overlap with the above list.)

1

INFLUENCES ON WORSHIP

First World War — Liturgical Movement — Charismatic Movement

Missionary Movement — WORSHIP — Ecumenical Movement

New technology — ? — 'Post-modernism'

2

NEW THINKING ABOUT WORSHIP

BCP

UNIFORMITY
'These bricks, in this order, in every place, every time'
'local church' = national church

ASB

FLEXIBILITY
'Mainly these bricks, in roughly this order, in most places, most weeks'

CW

FLEXIBILITY & VARIETY
'Bricks (including these), in some order'
'local church' = congregation

3

ROOTS OF CHRISTIAN WORSHIP: THE LAST HUNDRED YEARS

1912 – Appointment of the Advisory Committee on Liturgical Questions. It had very limited terms of reference, lasted but a few years and little of its work was acted upon.

1914–1918 – Experience of Chaplains in First World War confirms that Church of England liturgy is no longer relevant or familiar to large parts of the population.

Growth of 'Parish Communion' services.

1949 – First conference of Parish and People Movement.

1955 – First 'standing' Liturgical Commission appointed.

1966 – *Alternative Services Series 1*.

1967–68 – *Alternative Services Series 2*, the first prepared by the Liturgical Commission.

1973–79 – *Alternative Services Series 3*, the first to use modern language.

1980 – *The Alternative Service Book*.

1986 – *Lent, Holy Week, Easter*.

1991 – *Promise of His Glory* (covers All Saints to Presentation of Christ).

1995 – *Patterns for Worship*.

1900s
1910s
1920s
1930s
1940s
1950s
1960s
1970s
1980s
1990s
2000s

1906 – Royal Commission concludes that, 'the law of public worship in the Church of England is too narrow for the religious life of the present generation'.

Publication of *The English Hymnal*, specifically designed to provide hymnody to fit in with Anglican liturgical requirements.

1928–29 – Attempt to revise BCP rejected by Parliament.

1945 – Publication of *The Shape of the Liturgy* by Gregory Dix. Profoundly formed subsequent thinking.

1963 – Formation of the ecumenical Joint Liturgical Group (JLG).

1967 – Publication of the *Constitution on the Sacred Liturgy*, one of the first results of the Second Vatican Council.

1960s & 70s – Growth of 'Family' Services.

1982 – Publication of first edition of *Hymns for Today's Church*; the first hymnbook to attempt a thorough updating of 'archaic' language in hymns.

1988 – The General Synod report *Making Women Visible* suggests ways of incorporating 'inclusive language' into ASB services.

2000 – *Common Worship* main Sunday book and *Common Worship: Pastoral Services* published.

THE CHRISTIAN YEAR

PART A – GETTING STARTED

Aim

To explore some of the ways in which the Church's calendar assists our celebration of the Christian faith.

Leader's preparation

Make sure you have had a look at the *Common Worship* calendar (within *Calendar, Lectionary and Collects*, Church House Publishing, 1997), including the section of the Liturgical Commission's commentary (pp. 241–246) concerned with the calendar. The calendar (but not the commentary) is also included in *Common Worship: Services and Prayers for the Church of England* (p.1).

Opening worship

Sing the hymn 'We have a gospel to proclaim', or another hymn or song that features several parts of the Church's calendar.

Read Ecclesiastes 3.1–8 and then keep a time of silence for reflection.

After the silence, conclude the worship with the following prayer:

> O God, by whose command the order of time runs its course:
> forgive our impatience, perfect our faith,
> and, while we wait for the fulfilment of your promises,
> grant us to have a good hope because of your word;
> through Jesus Christ our Lord. **Amen.**

David Silk, based on prayer by Gregory Nazianzen

Session starter

Share with one another your favourite days in the Church's worship.
(See Session 2 – Before the next session)

How does your church prepare for these special days?

Does the liturgy used in your church on these days reflect the way you feel?

PART B – HEART OF THE MATTER

See pages 26–30

Advent

PART C – TAKING IT FURTHER

For further discussion

How would a visitor to your church discover what part of the Christian Year was being celebrated

❖ at a service of worship?

❖ when no service was going on?

Reading and resources

Michael Perham, *Celebrate the Christian Story* (SPCK, 1997). A good introduction to the *Common Worship* calendar with its associated lectionary and collects.

Mark Earey, *Lectionary Training Pack* (*Praxis*, 1997). OHP masters and leader's notes to help explain the principles behind the *Common Worship* calendar and lectionary.

Michael Perham and Kenneth Stevenson, *Waiting for the Risen Christ* and *Welcoming the Light of Christ*. Two books that accompany the commended resource books *Lent, Holy Week, Easter,* and *The Promise of His Glory*, each providing a theological and historical background to its respective services and some practical suggestions for using the material.

Thomas Talley, *Origins of the Liturgical Year* (Pueblo, 1986). A detailed and thorough study which has proved very influential.

Closing worship

Using resource books such as *Patterns for Worship*, *Enriching the Christian Year* or *Celebrating Common Prayer,* construct a short act of worship featuring material for the liturgical season you are in. If in 'Ordinary Time', choose an alternative theme such as 'Kingdom', 'Family', or 'Peace'.

You may find the following structure useful:

An opening prayer (which may accompany the lighting of a candle)
A seasonal reading
A form of intercession

At the end of the worship keep a short time of silence to give thanks for the riches of the Christian year.

Conclude by singing a seasonal hymn, or, if in Ordinary Time, 'The day thou gavest' or 'Lord of all hopefulness'.

Before the next session

What is your favourite Bible passage, and why?

In what context was your first encounter with the Bible (e.g., reading it at home, hearing it at church, studying it at school in RE, and so on)?

PART B – **HEART OF THE MATTER**

WHY KEEP THE CHRISTIAN YEAR?

The Christian year, sometimes called the Church's calendar, provides a framework for our Christian journey, both as individuals and as a Church. Its structure helps us make sense of our experience together.

❖ It is a way of **teaching** the faith, as we focus on one particular part of the Christian story – the coming of Jesus as a baby and at the end of all things, or his ministry of preaching and healing and teaching, or his sufferings and death, or his resurrection and ascension, or the coming of the Holy Spirit. All these wonders are true all the time, as we remember when we say the Creed at any service. But because human beings find it difficult to take in the whole picture in one sweep, it may help our Christian journey if we concentrate on one aspect of the faith at a time.

❖ It allows us to **make connections** between the rhythms of our own lives, with their high points and their times of difficulty, and the rhythm of the life of Jesus and of his Church, a rhythm with its own changes of mood. Sometimes our mood will be reflected in the mood of the Church's year; at other times the mood of the liturgy may challenge us and help to strengthen us in our faith.

❖ It recognizes the importance to us of the **natural seasons** and our human urge to celebrate **anniversaries** as the years go round (see Visual 1). Christians, in common with those of many religions, see a God-given order in the seasons, as reflected in the first creation account in Genesis where the sun and moon are given to the world to be 'for signs and for seasons and for days and years' (Genesis 1.14). But while the religions of the East often understand reality as being a cycle where life goes round and round until we manage to escape from it, Christians believe that life is a journey that is going somewhere – a straight line, rather than a circle. Yet we are also aware of the passing of the years, of the way that winter turns to spring, and of the special anniversaries of our own lives, whether happy or sad. The Christian year helps us to think in the same cyclic way about our faith. But because we are on a journey, the circular pattern becomes more like a spiral, where each year takes us round and forward at the same time.

THE DEVELOPMENT OF THE CHRISTIAN YEAR

There are four basic elements to the Christian year as it developed in the early Church, and as it is reflected in the Church of England calendar. (SEE VISUAL 2)

1 Celebrating death and resurrection

Good Friday and **Easter Day** are at the heart of the Church's life, as Christians share through their worship in the death and resurrection of Christ. In the early Church it was customary for baptisms to take place at Easter, as well as for those who had been separated through sin from the Church's fellowship to be restored to full communion. Those to be baptized or restored to fellowship kept a time of preparation for Easter, which we know as **Lent**, and later this season of Lent was observed by all Christians. Easter Day extends into **Eastertide** – a fifty-day season of joyful reflection on the resurrection of Jesus until the coming of the Holy Spirit on the day of **Pentecost**.

2 Celebrating the incarnation

The festival of **Christmas** was not fixed in its present form until the fourth century, when it may have taken over the pagan festival of the winter solstice. The same is true of **The Epiphany**, the Christmas festival in the Eastern Church, where the solstice was celebrated on 6th January. In the Western Church, including the Church of England, the two festivals were brought into association with each other, with Christmas celebrating the birth of Christ, and The Epiphany the showing of his glory to the world. Towards the sixth century **Advent** had evolved as a preparation both for Christmas and for the return of Christ in glory. The incarnation cycle ends after forty days of celebration with the Feast of **The Presentation of Christ in the Temple** ('Candlemas') on February 2nd.

3 Celebrating the heroes of the faith

The early Christians often kept the anniversaries of local martyrs; men and women whose heroic example was an inspiration to those who came after them. It also became the custom to remember other great figures from Christian history, as a reminder that we are one living fellowship across space and time. In particular, the celebration of those men and women who had

> **DISCUSSION**
> Invite the group to name those men and women from the Church's history who are particularly significant for them. How can we most effectively celebrate them in the Church today?

known Jesus in his earthly life, and foremost among them his mother, the Blessed Virgin Mary, became an important feature in the Christian calendar.

4 Celebrating God's goodness everyday

It seems likely that as well as keeping the great festal periods and the celebration of the saints, the early Church thought of the remainder of the year in a different way. There was no particular seasonal emphasis on which to focus during this period of 'Ordinary Time' (as we call it today), but from the earliest days of the Church, Sunday was kept every week as a celebration of the resurrection of Christ that was at the heart of the Gospel, while the readings during Ordinary Time tended to concentrate on the ministry and teachings of Christ and the early Church.

In addition to the rhythms provided by the principal seasons of the Christian year, each day contained its own rhythm too. While the observance of Sunday provided for a weekly celebration of the resurrection, daily prayer provided a way of remembering the incarnation of Christ, as the goodness of God was celebrated through the ordinary rhythms of daily life. See Visual 3

❖ As the sun rises, the morning hymn of praise *Benedictus* (the Song of Zechariah – Luke 1.68–79) promises the coming of Christ the light into the midst of his people.

❖ At the end of the day's work, *Magnificat* (the Song of Mary – Luke 1.46–55), celebrates that, as the world was at its evening, a new act of God's creation was begun in the womb of Mary.

❖ At the close of the day, *Nunc dimittis* (the Song of Simeon – Luke 2.29–32) invokes the Master's blessing of protection and peace on all those who have seen and celebrated his presence during the day that is past.

DISCUSSION
At what time of day do you find it easiest/hardest to pray?

Which of the daily canticles (Benedictus, Magnificat, Nunc dimittis) best captures the mood of: (a) your own spirituality? (b) the spirituality of your church?

THE CALENDAR TODAY

The *Common Worship* calendar shows clearly the two annual cycles centred on Christmas and Easter, with periods of non-seasonal Ordinary Time in between. (See handout). The year begins with the season of **Advent**, a time of preparation for the second coming of Christ, and, especially from mid-December onwards, a kind of countdown to his first coming at Bethlehem. **Christmas Day** begins forty days of rejoicing at the birth of Christ, with the traditional twelve days of Christmas until the Epiphany 'a unity of days of special thanksgiving'. **The Epiphany** begins a season

in which the revelation of Christ's glory is celebrated not only in the story of the Magi, but also at his baptism and at the miracle of Cana when water was turned into wine. The season ends with the feast of **The Presentation of Christ** (Candlemas), a day both of rejoicing and of sorrow that comes at a kind of pivotal point in the Church's year. The Church looks back for the last time to Christmas, at the end of the forty days of gladness. At the same time, Christians look towards suffering ahead. Even as the old man Simeon rejoices that in the child Jesus he has seen the salvation promised by God become a reality, he also declares that Jesus will be rejected and that a sword will pierce Mary's heart. These are some of the themes that will be taken up by the Church in the season of Lent that is drawing near. Before it arrives there is a short period of 'Ordinary Time' when there is no particular seasonal emphasis, although on the two Sundays before Lent the themes of creation and transfiguration begin to move us towards the solemn celebration that is to come.

Ash Wednesday begins the season of **Lent**, a season of preparation for Easter. Lent is not just about remembering the forty days spent by Jesus in the wilderness, although that is the theme of the readings on the First Sunday of Lent. The account of the temptations of Christ is an example of the self-discipline and denial to which all Christians are called as they walk with Jesus in the way of the cross. Worship during this period is often characterized by restraint and simplicity in contrast to the joy of Easter that lies ahead.

DISCUSSION
How can the Church's worship during Lent reflect a spirit of restraint and simplicity? (Omitting 'Alleluia' and doing without flowers are two common features – see below – but are there other ways?)

How can we celebrate Mothering Sunday (The Fourth Sunday of Lent) in a positive way without losing that Lenten spirit?

With the Fifth Sunday of Lent, **Passiontide** begins, and the theme of the liturgy begins to focus more closely on the death of Jesus on the cross. **Palm Sunday** is the first day of **Holy Week**, which leads through **Maundy Thursday** and **Good Friday** to the most important day of the Christian Year, **Easter Day**; the celebration of the resurrection of Christ, and the beginning of **Eastertide** which continues for fifty days. After forty days a new dimension is added as the **Ascension** of Christ is celebrated, and the following nine days prepare the Church to recall the sending of the Holy Spirit on the day of **Pentecost** (or Whitsunday), the last day of Eastertide.

Beginning on the weekdays after the Day of Pentecost and for the rest of the year the Church returns to Ordinary Time. The Sunday after the Day of Pentecost is celebrated as **Trinity Sunday**, and the Sundays which follow are designated as Sundays after

Trinity. They are not described as Sundays 'of' Trinity, for they do not constitute a kind of Trinity season, as Ordinary Time is to be seen as a non-seasonal period.

Although Ordinary Time extends until Advent begins once more, the month of November (the Sundays before Advent) is treated rather differently to allow reflection on the reign of Christ in earth and heaven. **All Saints' Day**, which is celebrated either on November 1st or the Sunday closest to it, begins this period, while **Christ the King** brings it and the whole Christian year to a fitting climax. Within this period of reflection comes an optional **Commemoration of the Faithful Departed** (sometimes called All Souls' Day) when Christians can remember those who have died who were known to them, and celebrate the unity in Christ of the Church living and departed. **Remembrance Sunday** provides another opportunity for similar reflection in the light of both the horrors and the self-sacrifice of human conflict.

DISCUSSION

In small groups list on a large sheet of paper the events that are significant in your church and community in the October and November part of autumn. Talk together about the feelings, images and words that you associate with this time of year and these events, and record these also on the sheets of paper. Share the results with everyone else.

CELEBRATING THE CHRISTIAN YEAR

There are many ways to enrich our celebration of the Christian year and many resources available to help us do it: e.g. *Patterns for Worship* (Church House Publishing 1995), Michael Perham ed. *Enriching the Christian Year* (SPCK, 1993) and the forthcoming book on *Times and Seasons* in the *Common Worship* series. (SEE VISUAL 4)

Seasonal words

❖ During the seasons, the **collects** and **lectionary readings** have a seasonal flavour, as they focus on those part of the Bible and the Christian tradition which are particularly associated with each season. (This will be developed further in Session 4.)

❖ During the Eucharistic Prayer, there may be a **seasonal Preface**. (See Session 9 for an explanation of this term.)

❖ At various other points in the service **optional seasonal material** may be used, for example:
Within the Prayers of Penitence
During the Intercessions
At the introduction to the Peace
At the Blessing
In the choice of Acclamations and other responsive texts
In the choice of Canticles at Services of the Word.

❖ Sometimes a seasonal flavour can be strengthened by the **omission** of certain texts.

In many churches care is taken to avoid the use of the word 'Alleluia' during Lent. Although 'Alleluia' is used throughout the year, it is particularly associated with the joy of Eastertide, and its omission during Lent helps to point up the contrast between the seasons. Some churches omit the joyful anthem 'Gloria in excelsis' at Holy Communion during Advent and Lent for the same reason.

Seasonal music

The choice of music is another major factor in helping to celebrate the distinctive seasons of the Christian year. It is obviously important to select hymns, songs and anthems, the words of which fit the seasonal theme, but the mood and style of the music itself also contribute to the overarching 'feel' of the worship. (See Session 5 for a fuller discussion of this.)

Seasonal colours

In some churches, different colours are used during the year for the vestments of the ministers, the frontals and the hangings at the pulpit and lectern. The pattern of colour usage varies from place to place, and any directions given in official liturgical books such as *Common Worship* are intended solely as a guide to those churches which wish to follow them. There are other well-established patterns (such as the Sarum Usage at Salisbury and elsewhere) but the one outlined here is the most common. (See handout)

❖ **White** or **Gold** – the colour of rejoicing and of purity – is used for the great festal periods of Christmas/Epiphany and Eastertide, and on any festivals of Our Lord, of the Blessed Virgin Mary, and of saints not venerated as martyrs.

❖ **Red** – the colour of blood, of fire, and of kingship – is used during Holy Week and of the festivals of martyrs, as well as on the Feast of Pentecost and for other services which focus on the gift of the Holy Spirit. It may also be used in the period before Advent between the feasts of All Saints and Christ the King as the Church reflects on the reign of Christ in heaven and on earth.

❖ **Purple** (or sometimes blue) – the colour of dignity and penitence – is used during the seasons of Advent and Lent. As an alternative during Lent, unbleached linen is used, recalling the sackcloth associated with repentance in the Old Testament.

❖ **Green** – the colour of growth – is used at all other times.

Flowers are another way in which the Christian year can be celebrated. Floral displays can be presented in colours which reflect the colours of the seasons elsewhere within the church, while the complete absence of flowers during Advent and Lent can help to add to the mood of restraint before the church is decorated for Christmas and Easter. Easter, with its seasonal readings about the empty tomb set in a Jerusalem garden, is a time when most

DISCUSSION

The above scheme for the use of liturgical colours is an arbitrary one which has developed over the centuries. If you were designing your own scheme, which colours would you use when, and why? You might like to use the handout to design your own colour scheme.

churches are filled with beautiful flowers, and many feature an Easter Garden which may provide a focus for special prayers and devotions during the Easter season.

Seasonal actions

Many of the important times of the Christian year have seasonal actions associated with them. Some of these have a long history while others are of more recent origin. As with all symbolic actions there is a danger that the original meaning of such an action may become obscured over the years, and eventually the action is performed out of habit, leading to rightful suspicion of meaningless ceremonial. But there will always be some symbolic objects and actions which retain the power to speak as loudly to us as the words of the liturgy, less precisely than words perhaps, but in a way that deepens through repetition, as we discover through the symbol new aspects of the mystery of God. When using such symbols, it may be important to provide some explanation as to their meaning, but care should be taken not to explain too much, or the symbol itself may be robbed of its power to speak in different ways to different people.

Here are some examples of such symbolic objects and actions from the seasons of the Christian year.

The **Advent wreath** is a ring of four red or purple candles in a ring around a white or gold candle. On each Sunday of Advent an additional candle from the ring is lit, and the central one on Christmas Day. The wreath provides a helpful way for children (and others!) to count down the Sundays before Christmas, while seasonal prayers linked with the lighting of the candles help to give an additional focus on the theme of the readings for each Sunday.

The **crib** is a familiar feature in many churches over the Christmas period, and it is often a focus for private prayer. There are several ways in which it may be used liturgically:

DISCUSSION

Advent is a season of preparation for judgement and the return of Christ, as well as for Christmas. How can you keep Advent in an age that begins to celebrate Christmas at the beginning of October if not before?

❖ At a crib service on Christmas Eve, where the children help the minister to arrange the figures in the crib.

❖ At a Holy Communion service at midnight, when the figure of the Christchild might be carried in procession and placed in the crib.

❖ As a place where the clergy and ministers might stop *en route* to their usual places for leading worship, for prayers (especially of penitence) to be said, or where children might gather to sing carols.

During **Epiphany**, the crib may help to emphasize the characteristic theme of the manifestation of Christ's glory to the world by adding the figures of the Wise Men to those already there, or even by replacing the figures of the shepherds with those of the Wise Men. Liturgical material is available for use at the presentation of the gifts of the Wise Men, as well as to celebrate the other Epiphany themes of the baptism of Christ and the changing of water into wine at Cana. As the Epiphany season extends until the Presentation, it would make liturgical sense for the crib to remain in place throughout January, possibly with some explanatory material available for those who think Christmas begins in November and ends by Boxing Day!

Another popular symbol often used during this part of the year is the **Christingle**, based on a custom from the Moravian Church of distributing lighted candles to children to celebrate the light of Christ. In its modern adaptation, the candle is held within an orange, representing the world, while cocktail sticks with fruits, sweets and nuts are added to represent the fruits of the earth, and a red ribbon is tied around the orange to represent the passion and death of Christ for the sake of the world.

The Feast of **The Presentation of Christ in the Temple** has traditionally been marked by a procession with candles (from which one of its alternative names 'Candlemas' is derived). In making the procession, the members of the congregation link their own lives with that of Christ, presenting themselves with him to do God's will. The procession also marks a turning point in the Christian year as all blow out their candles, and turn from the joy of Christmas and Epiphany to the darker days that lie ahead.

'Here we turn from Christ's birth to his passion.
**Help us, for whom Lent is near,
to enter deeply into the Easter mystery.'**

It is to help celebrate that Easter mystery that the Church has traditionally employed a large number of symbolic seasonal actions. Many of them are adaptations of ceremonies introduced by the Roman Catholic Church and traditionally associated within the Church of England with those churches described as 'Catholic' or 'High Church'. In recent years, however, many churches within a more Central or Evangelical tradition have begun to use and appreciate some of the dramatic actions described below, as have numerous congregations within the Free Church tradition.

Ash Wednesday derives its name from the ancient practice known as the **Imposition of Ashes**. During the Holy

Communion or some specially devised service of penitence, the members of the congregation may come forward and receive the sign of the cross in ash on their foreheads. It is a reminder both of our mortality, that we are dust and unto dust we shall return, and also of the source of our salvation, the cross, towards which our Lenten observance is leading. Some churches use last year's palm crosses, burnt to produce the ash.

Holy Week begins with the dramatic service of **Palm Sunday**. The Holy Communion on this day has two distinct moods. The first commemorates the entry of Jesus into Jerusalem. The members of the congregation gather, preferably in a place other than where the service will be celebrated, listen to the Gospel account of the triumphal entry, and then, waving palm branches and palm crosses, set off in procession, often singing 'All glory, laud and honour', as they accompany Jesus into the church, which becomes Jerusalem for the coming week. Once they have arrived, the mood changes abruptly for the long Passion Gospel, often read dramatically, as all present begin to face up to the demands of discipleship and experience how the easy 'Hosannas' soon give way to a sharing in the way of the cross.

Maundy Thursday is the day on which Christians remember the Last Supper Jesus shared with his disciples and give thanks that he is still known in the breaking of the bread. (See Sessions 8 and 9.) In the account of that last evening as told in the Fourth Gospel, Jesus also leaves another sign by which he will be remembered, as he rises from table, lays aside his outer garment, takes a bowl of water and begins to wash the disciples' feet. Provision is made for this act of service to be re-enacted within the liturgy of Holy Week, for example, by the presiding minister washing the feet of a representative group from amongst the congregation.

After the meal Jesus leaves the fellowship of the meal table to go out into the night to the garden of Gethsemane. In some churches an area of the building is set aside to represent the garden, and members of the congregation are encouraged to keep watch there with Jesus. Meanwhile the other areas of the church may be stripped of all their hangings and furnishings, as a sign of dereliction and abandonment. All leave in silence.

The liturgy of **Good Friday** emphasizes the reality of the cross. In many churches a large cross is brought into the assembly and set up at the front of the church as a focus for prayer and devotion. There are different traditions concerning the celebration of Holy Communion on this day. For some Christians, on Good Friday above all other days, it is felt to be highly appropriate to eat the bread and drink the cup, and thereby proclaim the Lord's death until he comes. In many other churches there is a strong custom that Holy Communion should be given from the bread and wine (or just the bread) consecrated at the service of Maundy Thursday, the two services being seen as a unity. In other churches there is the practice of deliberately refraining from the sacrament on Good Friday, marking this one day out as a day of dereliction and desolation.

The **Easter Liturgy** as outlined in *Lent, Holy Week, Easter* consists of four main parts:

❖ A **Vigil** of watching and waiting, meditating on the mighty acts of God in the Scriptures, and praying until the time (e.g., dawn) when the resurrection is to be celebrated.

❖ **The Service of Light** proclaiming the resurrection in both spoken word and dramatic ceremony, the Easter candle symbolizing Christ, the light of the world, risen from the darkness of the grave. In many churches the members of the congregation hold candles which are lit from the Easter candle as it passes through the church.

❖ **Baptism**, intimately linked with Easter in the early centuries of the Church's history, or at least the **Renewal of Baptismal Vows**, as all affirm their union with Christ in his death and resurrection.

❖ **Holy Communion** – the natural and proper climax of the whole Easter Liturgy, as the people are sacramentally reunited with their risen Lord.

The 'Alleluias' that herald the joy of Easter are a characteristic feature in the worship that is to follow for the whole 50 days of Eastertide, while the Easter candle stands alight in a prominent position in the church reminding all who enter it that the Church's Lord has risen from the dead.

 DISCUSSION

From the list of symbols and actions above, do you have a favourite or one that speaks most powerfully to you? Explain your choice to the rest of the group.

Do you think that Holy Communion should be celebrated on Good Friday, distributed from the bread and wine consecrated on Maundy Thursday, or not celebrated at all?

The fifty days of Easter are an extended period of praise and rejoicing. How can you sustain that sense of joy in your worship over such a long period?

session 3 – **HANDOUT**

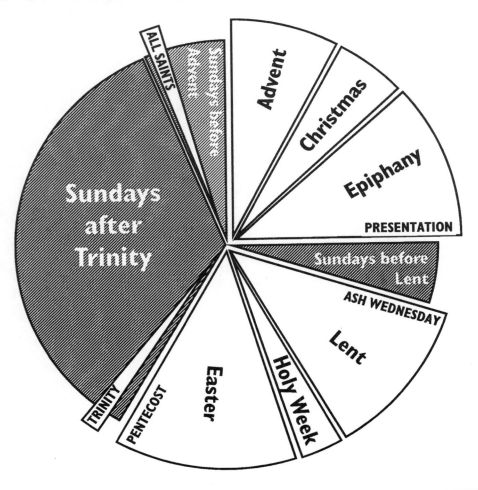

Advent

Christmas

Epiphany

PRESENTATION

Sundays before Lent

ASH WEDNESDAY

Lent

Holy Week

Easter

PENTECOST

TRINITY

Sundays after Trinity

ALL SAINTS

Sundays before Advent

COLOUR	TRADITIONAL SEASON/FOCUS	YOUR COLOUR	YOUR SEASON/FOCUS
Green	Ordinary Time		
White and/or Gold	Celebration, festivals of the Lord – e.g., Christmas, Epiphany, Easter – also Saints		
Purple	Penitence – e.g., Lent, Advent (may be replaced by sackcloth in Lent)		
Red	Pentecost, Spirit, Passiontide, Martyrs, and may be used in the period before Advent		

session 3 – VISUALS

1
WAYS OF UNDERSTANDING TIME

Cyclic

Linear

Spiral

2
FOUR ELEMENTS OF THE CHRISTIAN YEAR

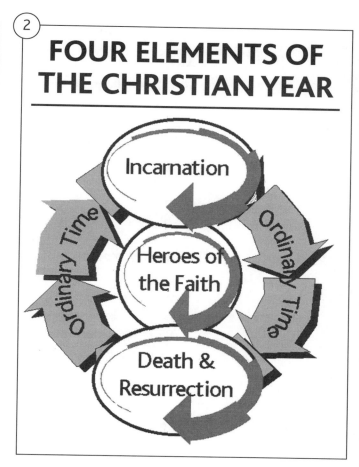

3
RHYTHMS OF DAILY PRAYER

Benedictus

Nunc Dimittis

Magnificat

4
CELEBRATING THE SEASONS

Words

Music

Colour

Actions

THE WORD OF GOD IN WORSHIP

PART A – GETTING STARTED

Aim

To explore the place of Scripture in the worship of the Church and the role of the lectionary in structuring the Church's engagement with the word of God.

Leader's preparation

Have a large Bible (and possibly a candle and matches) ready for the act of worship.

Make sure you have had a look at the *Common Worship* lectionary (*Calendar, Lectionary and Collects,* Church House Publishing, 1997), including the section of the Liturgical Commission's commentary (at the back) concerned with the lectionary.

Opening worship

Begin by placing a large open Bible in the centre of the group, or in a prominent place. If appropriate, place a lighted candle close to it.

Use the responses printed on the handout.

Read (or ask one of the group to read) Psalm 19. Leave a pause for reflection.

One or more of the following songs and hymns might be used either here or in the closing worship. If the group is not up to singing, then you may be able to find recordings of these or other suitable songs or music, or the words may be used for prayer or meditation:

❖ Lord, thy word abideth (H. W. Baker)

❖ Thanks to God whose Word was spoken (R. T. Brooks)

❖ Lord, I have made thy word my choice (Isaac Watts)

❖ Thy word is a lamp unto my feet (Amy Grant and Michael W. Smith)

Other appropriate Bible passages which might be used in addition to or in place of Psalm 19 include:

❖ 2 Timothy 3.14–17 ('all scripture is God-breathed');

❖ Nehemiah 8.1–12 (Ezra and the scribes read the law to the people);

❖ 2 Kings [22.3–10] 23.1–3 (Josiah reads the book of the covenant);

If possible leave the Bible open and the candle burning throughout the session.

Session starter

Ask group members to share with the rest of the group (or in ones and twos):

❖ What is their favourite passage in the Bible, and why?

❖ In what context was their first encounter with the Bible (e.g., reading it at home, hearing it at church, studying it at school in RE, and so on)?

Reflect on any pattern which emerges from the favourite passages shared (e.g., Are they mainly New Testament or Old? Predominantly Gospel passages, stories or 'teaching'? And so on). Reflect in the large group on how our first encounters with the Bible form our assumptions about it. For instance, if we first encounter it read aloud in church do we think of the Bible differently to the way we might think of it if we first encounter it as a book that we read alone?

PART B – HEART OF THE MATTER

See pages 36–9

PART C – TAKING IT FURTHER

For further discussion

Thinking about the Sunday worship in your church, in what ways do the following highlight (or fail to highlight) the significance of the Scripture readings:

❖ the shape and structure of the service. Do the readings get lost, or are they clearly significant?

❖ the use of music and singing?

❖ the use of ceremonial?

❖ the use of a clear 'place' for the ministry of the Word, analogous to the holy table for the ministry of the Sacrament?

Could any of these be used better?

Do you think it is better to encourage people to listen to the readings without the words in front of them, or to follow them in Bibles, lectionary or printed sheets? Are there circumstances when you would decide differently?

Can you think of any implications for the training of those who read the Bible in services?

Reading and resources

Michael Vasey, *Reading the Bible at the Eucharist* (Grove Books Worship Series No. 94, 1986) – a brief introduction to the development, value and use of lectionaries in the reading of Scripture.

Michael Perham, *Celebrate the Christian Story* (SPCK, 1997) – a guide to the *Common Worship* lectionary and how it fits in with the calendar.

Fritz West, *Scripture and Memory: the Ecumenical Hermeneutic of the Three-Year Lectionary* (The Liturgical Press, 1997) – a detailed look at how the three-year lectionary, in its various forms, works.

Normand Bonneau, *The Sunday Lectionary: Ritual Word, Paschal Shape* (The Liturgical Press, 1998) – a history of lectionaries and the emergence of the three-year *Lectionary for Mass.*

Horace Allen and Joseph Russell, *On Common Ground* (Canterbury Press, 1998) – a history of the Revised Common Lectionary.

Mark Earey, *Lectionary Training Pack* (Praxis, 1997) – a practical exploration of the philosophy behind the three-year lectionary and the practical implications of using it.

Closing worship

See above under 'Opening Worship' for suggested hymns and songs.

If you include prayers of intercession you could pray for Bible translators, preachers and those who read the Bible in church, those who write and publish Bible reading notes.

Use the Collect on the handout (Collect for the Last Sunday after Trinity). If you prefer to use the Prayer Book form, you'll find it as the Collect for the Second Sunday in Advent.

Before the next session

❖ Choose three of your favourite hymns or songs and be ready at the next session to say why they are your favourites.

❖ What do you like and dislike about your church building?

PART B – **HEART OF THE MATTER**

THE LITURGY OF THE WORD

The Liturgy (or Ministry) of the Word has two key parts: the reading of one or more passages from the Bible and the preaching of a sermon.

In some churches the focus is most naturally on the reading of the Bible itself (particularly the Gospel reading, which may be emphasized by the use of music, symbol and action, such as the use of incense, candles, or a procession). The sermon may be little more than a brief homily. In other traditions the focus is on the sermon, and the reading of the Bible is essential, but secondary to that.

The Church of England has a long tradition of using scriptural texts and biblical imagery in all its liturgy, but the Liturgy of the Word is where our relationship to the Scriptures is most clearly focused and expressed.

In the context of an act of worship the reading of the Scriptures is itself a significant action. It is both practical and symbolic:

❖ **practical** because it means that we hear at least a part of the Bible read each week;

❖ **symbolic** because it reminds us that our whole life, corporately and individually, is lived in the light of God's Word.

At one level a lectionary is simply a list of Bible passages assigned to be read on given days of the year. At a deeper level, a lectionary is a tool to help the Church to engage with the Word of God in a structured way. A lectionary is part of the context in which the Word of God is heard and understood and, as such, it has an impact on the interpretation of that Word.

N.B. The Church of England does not prescribe which translation of the Bible should be used. This decision is taken at the local level. The books which we sometimes call 'lectionaries' consist of readings from the lectionary printed out in full, using a particular Bible translation such as the New Revised Standard Version (NRSV) or the New International Version (NIV). This applies equally to the decision about which version of the Psalms to use for saying or singing. The Common Worship material includes a new translation of the Psalms, but this is not compulsory – any translation may be used. This is important where a church wishes to use a particular musical setting for the Psalms.

WHAT DOES READING THE BIBLE IN WORSHIP DO TO SCRIPTURE?
[SEE VISUAL 1 – SCRIPTURE 'TRAJECTORY']

Whenever we take a passage from the Bible and use it in worship we are putting it into another context and hence we change the way it is heard and understood.

It begins its life in its biblical context: the part of the Bible (Old Testament or New Testament), the book of the Bible, the place within that book (including what precedes and follows it), the genre of literature into which it falls, and so on.

This Bible context is the starting point, but in an act of worship it will not be the finishing point. Between biblical context and the mind of the hearer, the Bible passage will go through various filters that will influence greatly the way it is finally understood and applied.

Seasonal context

First, the passage is put into a seasonal context – including both 'church' seasons and 'natural' seasons. For instance, if you read, 'For to us a child is born, to us a son is given' in December, it is likely to be heard as referring to Christ. As part of a sermon series on Isaiah in the middle of July, it will be heard and understood differently: its historical context and its place and relevance within the whole Bible will be more prominent in the way it is interpreted. Passages about death and eternal life feel different in the dark days of autumn to the way they feel in the spring.

Worship context

Then, is this a service of Holy Communion, a non-eucharistic Word-focused service, a baptism, an all-age service, or an outreach service? Is it morning or evening? Is the average age of the congregation sixteen or sixty? All these things will affect the way a Bible passage is heard, understood and preached on. The story of the crossing of the Red Sea will be used and heard one way in a baptismal service and another way in a sermon series on Exodus. 1 Corinthians 13 will be applied one way in a wedding service and another way in Sunday school.

Corporate context

The next filter is the current corporate experience of the congregation. The story of Jesus welcoming the children would be heard as an encouragement to a church planning a summer holiday club for local children, but would strike different chords in a community facing the death of a child from cancer.

Personal context

Finally the passage reaches the filter of the individual hearers. They may be new believers or lifelong Christians. Some of them will be grieving or sad or angry; others may be experiencing times of great personal joy, growth and fulfilment. The Bible passage will be heard against this background.

This process is inevitable: texts need a context in order to be understood. Biblical texts often have many levels of meaning and are rightly approached differently in different circumstances.

Who makes the decisions?

Some denominations assume that the local church or the particular preacher or worship leader should choose Bible readings. In other churches, decisions about Bible readings are taken at a denominational, a national or an international level. But the 'trajectory' will happen whichever way the readings are chosen. Churches that base the choice of readings on a lectionary are simply doing the choosing in a long-term and very deliberate way, and in a way that shares the decision-making with the Church beyond the local congregation. Lectionaries particularly engage with the first two filters: the seasonal and worship contexts.

WHY USE A LECTIONARY AT ALL?
Two sorts of ordered Bible reading

The early Christians seem to have continued the Jewish synagogue approach of a double pattern of Scripture reading:

❖ a lectionary for special days and seasons, with a particular focus (and where the readings were chosen to support and aid that focus);

❖ an 'ordinary' lectionary, used at other times, where passages of Scripture were read through more or less continuously from week to week, without a controlling theme (sometimes called *lectio continua*).

The *Common Worship* lectionary adopts a similar two-strand approach.

Why use a lectionary?

❖ It is a way of organizing the reading of Scripture, in which decisions about what is read are subject to the corporate decision of the **wider church** rather than the preferences of individual preachers or congregational leaders.

❖ It is a means of **unity** among Christians when worshippers in different churches and different denominations are focusing on the same passages of Scripture on a given Sunday.

❖ It ensures a **full coverage of Scripture**. No lectionary includes every verse of the Bible, but a lectionary is more likely to ensure that over time the whole message of the Scriptures is heard, and not merely favourite or well-known passages (or the minister's pet subject!).

❖ A lectionary enables some of the **long-term** thinking and planning of Bible reading to be done centrally and not reinvented in every worshipping community.

❖ Coupled with the church calendar, it ensures that all aspects of the **Gospel** are given proper attention.

DISCUSSION
[SEE HANDOUT QUESTION 2]

Imagine that this year there is to be only one service in your church over the Christmas period, with three Bible readings in it. Which three would you choose, and what principles have governed your choice?

Reflect on the difficulties of balancing short- and long-term needs when it comes to choosing readings.

HISTORY OF THE THREE-YEAR LECTIONARY

The Roman Catholic Church has been using a three-year cycle of readings in its *Lectionary for Mass* since the 1970s. American and Canadian Protestant churches adopted and adapted the three-year pattern and produced the *Common Lectionary* (1983).

Further use led to more changes, including the provision of two Old Testament tracks for Ordinary Time. One of these tracks contains Old Testament readings which are related or linked to the Gospel reading in some way, and the other track contains Old Testament readings that follow on from week to week and are not connected to the Gospel reading (this is sometimes called 'semi-continuous' reading). This was the *Revised Common Lectionary* (RCL, 1992).

In 1997 the Church of England authorized a new lectionary, collects and calendar, basing the Principal Service lectionary on the RCL. The Anglican Churches of Scotland, Ireland and Wales have also adopted versions of the RCL. The new *Methodist Worship Book* (1999) includes the RCL. Many other Churches around the world have also opted for the RCL. Some of these Churches have made changes to it, but in general terms it is now possible to say that a large proportion of Christians of different denominations and in various countries are likely to be reading the same passages of Scripture on any given Sunday.

DISCUSSION
[SEE HANDOUT QUESTION 3]

Do you think that the use of a 'common' lectionary is significant or even important? What are the advantages and disadvantages of its use?

PUBLIC AND PRIVATE

[VISUAL 2]

Fritz West suggests a basic division in the Church (which he labels as 'Protestant' and 'Catholic') over the way that Scripture is understood. It is possible to see this divide reflected in the different traditions within the Church of England.

❖ In the 'Catholic' tradition, Scripture is understood as passed on primarily by the community hearing and remembering it (that is, the public use of Scripture in worship).

❖ In the 'Evangelical' tradition, Scripture is understood as passed on primarily in written form (that is, the printed Bible).

The writers of the New Testament expected that people would *hear* their words read out in a public meeting, not by reading them privately in a book. No one in the first century envisaged a situation where someone could have a personal copy of the Bible and read it alone. Encountering Scripture in this way, by *hearing,* is inherently corporate: there have to be at least two people involved – one to speak and one to hear. Many Bible passages only make proper sense when this corporate context is understood. For instance, the curious 'let the reader understand' in Mark 13.14 is a direction to the person reading out loud.

Catholics are used to this idea that we encounter Scripture primarily by *hearing* it in the context of worship. And because the Catholic tradition values the Eucharist as the usual form of worship, the readings tend to be heard and interpreted in a way that is Christ-centred and Eucharist-focused. Hence, within the Catholic tradition, the public *reading* of the Scriptures has been stressed as the proclamation of the word.

However, there are weaknesses in this approach. It is hard to get a sense of the flow of a story or of the immediate context of a passage. Bible passages risk being known only as 'soundbites' without a context.

Those from a more Evangelical tradition are more used to encountering Scripture by *seeing* it in the printed Bible. This has a lot to do with the convergence in the sixteenth century of religious reform and the new technology of printing. Evangelicals tend particularly to value the private study of Scripture at home and to have Bibles in the pews at church. The positive side of this is a deep knowledge of the Scriptures and a sense that the Bible is a book for the rest of the week as well as for church. The negative side is that Scripture can be privatized – we can feel that we own it as individuals rather than as part of God's people.

Those from an Evangelical tradition instinctively look for the biblical context for a passage, and a lectionary can feel like something that comes between them and the Bible (though, as we have seen, a series of contexts will always come between Bible passage and hearers, whichever way the passage is chosen).

Even if they use a lectionary, those in the Evangelical tradition tend to use it in a different way to those in the Catholic tradition: they might choose only one or two readings and they look for the proclamation of the word to take place in the *sermon* as much as in the reading.

The Evangelical encounter with the Bible as *book* may lead to a sense that the worship context for Scripture is secondary and the biblical context is primary. But it could be argued that the 'trajectory' actually begins further back, in a worship context. Before the Bible existed as one book Christians began to recognize some texts as having the stamp of God's authority, as being the 'Word of God'. From this initial recognition, in the context of meeting for worship, the 'Canon of Scripture' began to take shape.

DISCUSSION
[SEE HANDOUT QUESTION 4]

Which aspects of these so-called 'Evangelical' and 'Catholic' approaches to Scripture can you recognize in the way the Bible is used in your church?

Having it both ways

The ecumenical three-year Revised Common Lectionary (RCL) draws on both traditions. From the Catholic tradition come the provision of four readings (Old Testament, Psalm, New Testament, and Gospel) and the assumption that the Gospel reading is key. The lectionary is also strongly linked to the Christian year. Hence the 'worship context' and 'seasonal context' filters are applied consciously and clearly.

From the Evangelical tradition comes a valuing of the whole Bible and of semi-continuous reading, allowing Scripture to be heard on its own terms and providing more of a biblical context for readings over a series of Sundays.

BASIC PRINCIPLES OF THE *COMMON WORSHIP* LECTIONARY

Lectionary and calendar

The *Common Worship* lectionary is closely tied to the Church year (see Session 3). The lectionary is divided into two parts: readings for the seasonal parts of the year, and readings for what is sometimes called 'Ordinary Time' (see Session 3, diagram on handout).

The three years of the lectionary

[SEE HANDOUT]

The lectionary has a three-year cycle. Each year focuses on one of the first three Gospels – Matthew in Year A, Mark in Year B and Luke in Year C.

The Gospel of the year is used in two ways:

❖ during **seasonal** time appropriate passages are chosen;

❖ in **Ordinary** Time passages follow on from Sunday to Sunday semi-continuously.

John's Gospel is used in all three years, particularly before and after Easter.

The lectionary readings [SEE VISUAL 3]

The **Gospel** is the starting point. The **New Testament** passages are independent of the Gospel reading and usually semi-continuous (even in seasonal time). For example, in the Sundays of Easter there are a series of readings from 1 Peter in Year A, 1 John in Year B and Revelation in Year C. In seasonal time the book chosen may reflect the feel of the season.

Old Testament passages are used in two ways:

❖ in the **seasons** they relate to the **Gospel**.

❖ in **Ordinary Time** you can **choose** either a 'continuous reading' track which takes you through a book week by week, or a 'Gospel-related' track which has OT passages which relate to the Gospel.

In Eastertide there is no OT reading – instead the book of Acts is used (though a table of OT readings is supplied if these are preferred).

Psalms are generally linked with the OT reading (and therefore where there are two possible OT readings there are two possible Psalms).

Other lectionary points

There are no themes to link the readings for each Sunday, and no Sunday theme titles (such as the 'Christ the Healer' etc. of the ASB). Instead, there is a multi-layered approach (VISUAL 4):

❖ a Gospel 'flavour' for the year;

❖ a seasonal focus where appropriate;

❖ scriptural continuity from week to week.

The 'Principal Service' provision is intended to be used for the main service of the day, whatever form that service takes (Holy Communion, Service of the Word, Morning Prayer, Evening Prayer, etc.) There are also two other lectionaries, for a Second and Third Service.

The Collects

The Collect prayers provided with the *Common Worship* lectionary are not tightly thematic, nor are they linked to the Bible readings. Hence the Collects work on a one-year cycle while the readings are on a three-year cycle. The intention is that the Collects come round frequently enough to become familiar and memorable.

'Closed' and 'open' seasons

[SEE SESSION 3, DIAGRAM ON HANDOUT]

The *Common Worship* lectionary allows for both commonality and local flexibility. It defines a 'closed season' as follows:

❖ First Sunday of Advent to The Presentation of Christ (Candlemas)

❖ Ash Wednesday to Trinity Sunday.

Outside these 'closed seasons' and 'after due consultation with the PCC, the minister may, from time to time, depart from the lectionary provision for pastoral reasons or preaching or teaching purposes' (Notes to the lectionary).

The provisions of *A Service of the Word* reduce the 'closed season' for non-eucharistic services, as follows:

❖ Advent 3 to The Baptism of Christ;

❖ Palm Sunday to Trinity Sunday.

session 4 – HANDOUT

DISCUSSION QUESTIONS

1. Sometimes the person reading the Bible ends the reading with, 'Here endeth the lesson,' or, 'Here ends the reading.' In recent years it has become more common to use the response, 'This is the word of the Lord./**Thanks be to God.**' Which do you prefer and why?

2. Imagine that this year there is to be only one service in your church over the Christmas period, with three Bible readings in it. Which three would you choose, and what principles have governed your choice?

3. What are the advantages and disadvantages of a 'common' lectionary? Do you think having a common lectionary is significant or even important?

4. Which aspects of the 'Evangelical' and 'Catholic' approaches to scripture (as described in this session) can you recognize in the way the Bible is used in your church?

> In the context of an act of worship the reading of the Scriptures is itself a significant action. It is both practical and symbolic: practical because it means that we hear at least a part of the Bible read each week; symbolic because it reminds us that our whole life corporately and individually is lived in the light of God's word.

> At one level a lectionary is simply a list of Bible passages assigned to be read on given days of the year. At a deeper level, a lectionary is a tool to help the Church to engage with the word of God in a structured way.

> . . . in general terms it is now possible to say that a large proportion of Christians of different denominations and in various countries are likely to be reading the same passages of Scripture on any given Sunday.

THE THREE YEARS OF THE LECTIONARY

Year A (e.g. Advent 2001– Advent 2002)	**Matthew**	**John**
Year B (e.g. Advent 2002– Advent 2003)	**Mark**	– used in all three years in the time before and after Easter
Year C (e.g. Advent 2000– Advent 2001)	**Luke**	

The Gospel of the year is used in two ways:
• during **seasonal** time appropriate passages are chosen;
• in **Ordinary** Time passages follow on from Sunday to Sunday semi-continuously.

OPENING WORSHIP

Your word is a lamp to my feet
and a light to my path.

How I love your law! It is my meditation all day long.
**Your word is a lamp to my feet
and a light to my path.**

CLOSING WORSHIP

(COLLECT FOR THE LAST SUNDAY AFTER TRINITY)

Blessed Lord,
who caused all holy scriptures to be written for our
    learning:
help us so to hear them,
to read, mark, learn and inwardly digest them
that, through patience, and the comfort of your holy
    word,
we may embrace and for ever hold fast
the hope of everlasting life,
which you have given us in our Saviour Jesus Christ,
who is alive and reigns with you,
in the unity of the Holy Spirit,
one God, now and for ever. Amen.

Before the next session

❖ Choose three of your favourite hymns or songs and be ready at the next session to say why they are your favourites.

❖ What do you like and dislike about your church building?

① SCRIPTURE 'TRAJECTORY'

Calendar

Worship

Corporate

Personal

② HAVING IT BOTH WAYS

'Catholic' model	'Protestant' model
Scripture as spoken word	Scripture as book
• Seasonally focused • Gospel-controlled • Christ-centred • Reading is primary	• Biblical context • Values all scripture • Preaching primary

• Seasonally based (seasonal context)
• Gospel-led (but not dominated)
• Semi-continuous (biblical context)
• Two-track (to allow OT continuity)

③ THE LECTIONARY READINGS

Seasonal time		Ordinary time
Semi-continuous (with seasonal 'feel' if appropriate)	New Testament	Semi-continuous
Chosen to suit season	Gospel	Semi-continuous
Gospel-related	Old Testament	Gospel-related *or* Semi-continuous
	Psalm	

④ A MULTI-LAYERED APPROACH

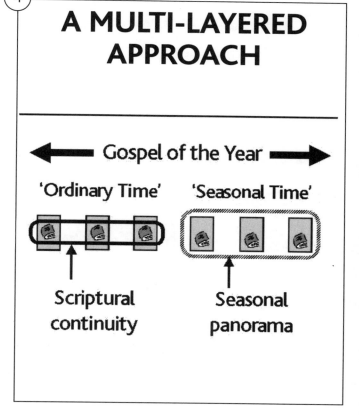

◄ Gospel of the Year ►

'Ordinary Time'   'Seasonal Time'

Scriptural continuity   Seasonal panorama

BEYOND THE WORDS OF WORSHIP

PART A – GETTING STARTED

Aim
To understand more about the way music, architecture and the senses contribute to worship.

Leader's preparation
Try to get hold of a plan of your church building as background for the discussion during the session starter. Alternatively produce your own plan.

Opening worship
Sing a hymn or song about the place of music and/or architecture in worship, e.g., 'Angel voices, ever singing' or 'We love the place, O God'.

❖ Read 1 Peter 2.4–10.

❖ Keep a time of silence.

❖ Use the *Common Worship* Collect for a Dedication Festival. Unless you are meeting in the church building, change 'this house of prayer' to 'our house of prayer', 'worship you here' to 'worship you there', and 'in this place' to 'there'.

Session starter
Discuss the questions you were asked to think about in preparation for this session. During your discussion of the second question, use a large sheet of paper to list your likes and dislikes about the church building.

PART B – HEART OF THE MATTER

See pages 43–7

PART C – TAKING IT FURTHER

For further discussion
Look again at your list of likes and dislikes with regard to your church building. Are there any you would now want to add or delete in the light of this session?

Using a large piece of paper produce, as a group, a plan of your perfect church.

Reading and resources
Richard Giles, *Repitching the Tent* (Canterbury Press, 2nd edition, 1999) – a fascinating study of the history, use and arrangement of church buildings and worship spaces.

In Tune with Heaven, the report of the Archbishops' Commission on Church Music (CHP, 1992) – a survey of the use of music in the Church of England in the closing years of the twentieth century with suggestions for future developments.

John Leach, *Hymns and Spiritual Songs: The Use of Traditional and Modern in Worship* (Grove, 1995) (Worship Series No. 132).

Paul Roberts, *Alternative Worship in the Church of England* (Grove, 1999) (Worship Series No. 155) – an introduction and description of so-called 'alternative worship', which often involves creative use of all senses in worship.

Closing worship
Use the prayer on the handout (adapted from *Enriching the Christian Year*). Share the leadership of the prayer around the group.

Before the next session
If you were determining a basic checklist of elements to include in a Sunday service that was not a Holy Communion, what would you include? Make it a list in two columns, one giving 'elements' of worship (for instance, things like 'a confession', 'a creed', 'the Lord's Prayer', 'the notices', 'hymns or songs') and one giving 'aspects' of worship (such as 'adoration', 'praise', etc.).

PART B – HEART OF THE MATTER

WORDS AND BEYOND WORDS

Much of the liturgical work of the Church of England in recent years has concentrated on the words of worship, the liturgical texts which go to make up *Common Worship* and the services which came before it. This is principally because the words used in worship have implications for doctrine and belief. There are three documents that make up the historic formularies of the Church of England, to which Anglican clergy assent when being licensed to a new parish: *The Thirty Nine Articles of Religion*, *The Book of Common Prayer* and *The Ordering of Bishops, Priests and Deacons*. It is significant that the last two of these three are liturgical texts.

But as human beings are more than the words which they utter, so worship is made up of many components beyond the words on the page of a service book. Christian worship often contains music and silence as well as speech; it is set in a particular location which makes its own impact on the service, and it is an activity which should involve the bodies as well as the minds of the worshippers.

MUSIC
History
Biblical foundations

It is clear from the Books of Chronicles (1 Chronicles 15.28; 16.42; 2 Chronicles 7.6; 29.25) that music played an important part in the worship of the Jerusalem temple. The Book of Psalms – the music book of that temple – abounds in references to music, and to a large array of instruments for performing it. (See, for example, Psalm 150). The first Christians continued to worship in the temple with its musical tradition, and in addition were encouraged to 'sing psalms and hymns and spiritual songs' when they met separately for Christian worship (Ephesians 5.19; Colossians 3.16). The younger Pliny, writing to the Emperor Trajan (AD 61–113), describes the practice of Christians to gather on stated days before sunrise and to sing 'a hymn to Christ as God'.

DISCUSSION

List the instruments and postures mentioned in Psalms 47, 81, 95, 98 and 150. Then make a list of the instruments and postures used in your normal main Sunday service. Compare the two lists and discuss.

Plainsong

The style of music which dominated Christian worship from about AD 400 to about AD 1500 was known as **plainsong** or **plainchant**, consisting of unaccompanied musical phrases sung in a free speech-like rhythm. The most comprehensive organization of these chants took place during the time of Pope Gregory the Great (590–604), and as a result this music is sometimes known as Gregorian chant.

After the Reformation in England, plainsong was adapted through the introduction of harmony and a more rigid framework into a style of singing that became known as **Anglican chant**, a method of singing Psalms and (sometimes) Canticles that is still frequently used in cathedrals and some churches.

The development of hymns

In continental Europe at the same time, Lutherans began to adapt some of the plainsong melodies into hymn-like compositions called **chorales** and to write words for them in their native language rather than Latin. These chorales were arranged according to a more rigid pattern of syllables (called a metre), and often had rhyming lines. (Two examples often sung today are 'A safe stronghold my God is still' and 'O sacred head, sore wounded'.)

Calvin and his followers set versions of the Psalms to fixed metres, and English versions of these **metrical psalms** are also part of contemporary hymnody (for example 'All people that on earth do dwell', usually sung to a Geneva tune, *The Old Hundredth*, and 'The Lord's my shepherd, I'll not want', sung to *Crimond*, a British tune composed on the same model).

During the eighteenth century many new hymns were produced by non-conformist writers, among them Isaac Watts and Charles Wesley, (the latter writing over 6000 hymns), and hymn singing became the characteristic music used in Protestant worship. With the publication of *Hymns Ancient and Modern* in 1861, many of the finest hymns from this tradition were made available for Church of England worship, together with fresh translations of hymns from earlier centuries.

Hymns and worship songs

Hymns (including worship songs) are one of the most familiar parts of Christian music to those who are not regular worshippers, and may serve several purposes.

❖ They **unite the worshippers**. Singing together helps to foster a sense of belonging and of 'team spirit'. Just as a crowd of football supporters reinforce their common identity through their team anthems, so hymns can unite a congregation in praise or in dedication.

❖ They **express Christian teaching** in a memorable way. With hymns especially, the combination of a singable tune and rhyming words written to fit a particular metre often makes hymns easier to memorize than the prose of the Bible or of liturgical texts.

❖ They **contribute to the mood** of an act of worship. The music can evoke various moods through the shape of its melodies, its harmonic structure (major or minor – simple or complex), its rhythms (smooth and foursquare, or syncopated and lively) and its dynamic contrasts (louds and softs), as well as by the choice of instruments or the stops used on the organ.

❖ They **help to pick up the seasonal or thematic emphasis** of a service to give a sense of coherence to the whole act of worship.

❖ They **assist the theological, devotional and/or practical flow** of a service. Sometimes hymns are used while a piece of liturgical action is taking place. In many churches, a hymn is sung while the holy table is prepared for Communion, and others may be used during the distribution.

DISCUSSION
Which of the above uses of hymns and worship songs do you think is the most important? Can you think of any other reasons for using hymns?

Hymns and Worship Songs – the differences
While the above points relate both to hymns and to worship songs, there are significant differences between these two types of composition. (See handout). Hymns and worship songs differ in whether they are sung *about* God or *to* God, as well as in their subject matter, length, durability, roots, accompaniment and other features.

DISCUSSION
What do you think are the strengths and weaknesses of the two types of composition? Which do you prefer singing, and why?

Choosing hymns and worship songs
The use of appropriate hymns is often a key component in making an act of worship as helpful and inspiring as possible. There are several reasons why a particular hymn may be the 'right' one for a given occasion:

❖ **Seasonal** – During the great seasons of the Church's year (see Session 3) the use of appropriate hymns can contribute to the seasonal 'feel' of a service. This may be particularly important during the festal seasons of Christmas/Epiphany and Easter, when joyful seasonal hymns can help sustain the sense of festivity.

❖ **Biblical** – Sometimes hymns are chosen because of a particular link with one or more of the readings of the day.

DISCUSSION
Which one hymn or song do you particularly associate with each of the following and why?

Advent
Christmas
Epiphany
Lent
Easter
Pentecost

The words may underline a point being made in a biblical passage, or use some of its images or theological terms. This can contribute greatly to the sense of cohesion of an act of worship, but should probably not be the only criterion used for choosing hymns. A service built around the Good Shepherd Gospel reading (John 10.11–18), for example, does not need to mention sheep and shepherds in every hymn!

❖ **Liturgical** – Hymns may be chosen because of their appropriateness for a particular part of the liturgy.

A hymn at or near the beginning of the service might well be one of praise and approach to God.
A hymn during the Liturgy of the Word could thank God for the gift of Scripture and ask that the hearers might be open to its teaching.
A hymn while the table is prepared might begin to reflect on the wonder of the love of God experienced through the communion.
A hymn at or near the end might be one of dedication to service.

❖ **Miscellaneous** – There are other factors which might be considered when choosing hymns:

Does the hymn help create or sustain the appropriate mood for that service (or part of the service)?
Is it the right length for that point of the service (if, for example, it will be sung while the collection is taken)?
Is there enough variety among the hymns chosen – of style, of metre, of composer?
Is there the right balance between well-known hymns (and especially tunes) and less familiar ones?

OTHER MUSIC FOR WORSHIP
Psalmody
The Psalms have always been a part of Christian worship, and one of the parts of the service most frequently sung, either set to plainsong or to Anglican chant, or by using a repeated refrain. (See Session 8 for a discussion of the Responsorial Psalm). Using Psalms helps to link today's Church with the Jewish roots of its worship.

Anthems and instrumental music

Music by an organist or music group before a service can help to create a worshipful atmosphere, while there may be opportunities for a choir or soloists to sing an anthem or other piece of music as an aid to devotion.

DISCUSSION
How much of the music in your church is sung by everyone and how much by a music group or choir? Do you think the balance is right?

Singing liturgical texts

There are further opportunities within the texts of the service themselves where the words can be sung rather than said. (See handout). Singing the liturgical texts themselves is a different way of using music in worship from that commonly found in Church of England or Free Church services. In Church of England worship the hymns have often been used as optional and additional elements inserted into a spoken liturgy, while in many Free Church services the hymns themselves have constituted the principal building blocks of the worship, with the said elements (readings, prayers, etc.) inserted between them. In modern Roman Catholic worship, and increasingly within Anglican worship too, music has come to be seen not as something which happens between the items of the liturgy, but as a way of enhancing those items, with the high points of the liturgy coinciding with the high points of the music. At Holy Communion, for example, there is a tradition in many churches of singing *Kyrie eleison, Gloria in excelsis*, some parts of the Eucharistic Prayer (especially 'Holy, holy, holy Lord', known by its Latin name *Sanctus*) and 'Lamb of God' or *Agnus Dei*. Many of the great European composers wrote settings for these parts of the service, as did the English composers of the last century.

Other parts of the service which could be sung might include:

* An Acclamation (often 'Alleluia') heralding the Gospel reading;

* Responses before and after the Gospel;

* Acclamations during the Eucharistic Prayer (and especially 'Christ has died' and its alternatives) (see Session 9 for details);

* The great 'Amen' at the end of the prayer;

* The Dismissal.

If the President is able to sing well these two might be added:

* The Collect (See Session 8);

* The whole of the Eucharistic Prayer.

DISCUSSION
❖ Which parts of the Communion service do you think should be sung, and why?

❖ Which of the patterns shown on the handout best describes the way music is used in your church?

Silence

The spaces between the words and the music are another important feature of worship that is sometimes overlooked. Some churches have a tradition of silent prayer before their Sunday service, but that may not always be possible or even desirable, in certain contexts. The justifiable demands of welcoming worshippers as they arrive and using music to create a particular mood of worship, and the likelihood that a number of the congregation will arrive flustered and/or late may mean that silence before the service is not easily an option. But it may be possible to make space for silent prayer at later points of the service (for example, before the Collect, during the Prayers of Intercession, and, if a Holy Communion service, after all have received.) Corporate silence can help to enable worshippers to make connections between their private prayers and the public worship of the Church.

DISCUSSION
Before the service starts in church do you think there should be silence, conversation, organ music, informal songs . . . or what? Give your reasons.

PLACE AND SPACE

Christian worship does not happen in a vacuum, but in a particular place, usually a church building. Buildings themselves express theology – usually the theology of those who built them, or who reordered or redesigned them over the centuries, which may or may not be the same as the theology as those who use them for their worship today.

The earliest days

The earliest Christian worship was usually celebrated in a private house, the shape and location of which differed throughout the Roman Empire. In the East, where buildings up to four storeys high were common, worship took place in the dining room which was usually on the top floor. In Rome, where many of the dwellings were tenements, with apartments horizontally across them, the largest chamber available would have been used.

State religion – basilicas [SEE VISUAL 1]

After the victory of Constantine, when Christianity became the state religion, worship became a public occasion, and churches were designed to reflect civic and imperial basilicas (large meeting halls). In general, basilica churches were single rooms, with an altar standing towards one end on the middle axis. This was the focal point of the building, and around it priests and laity gathered for the liturgy. By the middle of the fourth century the standard pattern was the altar at the eastern end, with the people facing eastwards and the clergy westwards.

The Middle Ages [SEE VISUAL 2]

During the Middle Ages the essential community element of the Eucharist began to be lost (see session 9) and the Mass became a ceremony performed by the clergy. The architectural patterns of the time reflect these changes. The place of the clergy was removed out of the body of the church to create a second room, the sanctuary. As the emphasis within the service shifted from receiving Communion to the consecration of the elements, at that moment the priest would elevate the host (consecrated bread) so that it could be glimpsed through the chancel screen beneath the rood (an image of the crucifixion) at the far end of the choir. The priest had also moved from facing the people across the altar to standing with his back to them, and so looking towards the East.

Eastern Orthodox Churches

Similar developments took place in the Eastern Orthodox Churches. By the late fourteenth century the clergy and the people were divided during the liturgy by a large screen (the iconostasis) on which were placed full-sized icons of the saints. This represented the veiling of heaven from earth, the saints depicted on the screen being mediators between the two realms. When the priest spoke from the altar behind the screen it was as if the voice of God was speaking to his people on earth. When the gates were opened and the ministers came forth from the altar to the people at the reading of the Gospel and the giving of Holy Communion, it was like the incarnation when Christ came forth from heaven to earth for the salvation of the human race.

The Reformation [SEE VISUAL 3]

The reformers rejected many of the medieval ideas about the Mass. They wished to emphasize the Communion aspect of the service, to lay stress on the place of the Bible and to break down the rigid division between ordained and lay. These theological emphases affected the way in which the existing medieval churches were adapted. The reformers decided to use the two rooms of the church for different functions. The nave was the place for the Liturgy of the Word and the sanctuary became the scene for the celebration of the Lord's Supper, the holy table being moved forward into the middle of the choir and the worshippers arranging themselves around it, with the minister standing at the North side and the congregation at the South.

The late twentieth century [SEE VISUAL 4]

In the Roman Catholic Church of the 1960s, the Second Vatican Council revolutionized both the Church's liturgy and also the architecture of the buildings in which this took place. These changes affected not just its own communion but many Anglican and Protestant Churches too. As in the days of the Roman basilicas, the presiding priest now faced the people westwards across the altar. The presidential role was emphasized by the placing of a prominent chair in which to sit when not at the altar. The lectern (the focus of the Liturgy of the Word) was given a new prominence, while the font was brought into the main body of the church as another focal point for liturgical action. The keynotes of late twentieth-century churches were simplicity and mobility – space to enable people to gather in various parts of the building, and several smaller rooms off the main building for the various activities – educational, administrative and social – of a busy modern church.

> ### DISCUSSION
>
> ❖ What theological message do you think is being given if for the Holy Communion the president faces: East (facing the same direction as the people and on their side of the holy table); West (behind the table facing the people)?
>
> Which do you prefer and why?
>
> ❖ If someone visited your church at a time when no service was in progress, what impression might s/he get from the arrangement of the building about the things your congregation thought important? (How important, for example, do the holy table, the pulpit, the lectern, the font appear?)

THE BODY IN WORSHIP

Posture

The services of *Common Worship* make some suggestions about posture. The notes which follow the Holy Communion service, for example, direct that all should stand for the Gospel, Creed, Peace and Dismissal; suggest that it may sometimes be appropriate to kneel for the Prayers of Penitence; and discourage any change of posture during the Eucharistic Prayer. Generally, however, decisions about when members of the congregation should stand, sit or kneel are a matter for local custom.

Kneeling, standing, sitting

The most common posture for prayer in the early Church was standing (often with arms outstretched – as in the catacomb paintings) especially as a way of marking Sundays as a weekly celebration of the resurrection. Standing is still the posture generally adopted in the Eastern Orthodox Churches today. It is likely that the change from standing to kneeling came about through the gradual omission of a command to rise after a short period appointed for silent kneeling prayer. This posture gradually spread to other parts of the service – at first in the Latin rite and from there into the early English rites. In the 1662 *Book of Common Prayer*, the faithful are ordered to kneel for the entire service except for the Gospel and the Creed. The introduction to the Confession spells it out clearly

'meekly kneeling upon your knees'.

What is being emphasized is our unworthiness to stand before God, we who

'are not worthy even to gather up the crumbs under thy table'.

(1662 BCP Prayer of Humble Access)

Compare those words with these from Eucharistic Prayer B of *Common Worship* Order One:

'. . . we thank you for counting us worthy
to stand in your presence and serve you'.

Christians praying in the third century in Rome (whose prayer forms the basis for part of this *Common Worship* prayer) wanted to emphasize their worthiness in Christ to stand before God, and their standing posture reflected that theology. As the priests mentioned in the Old Testament stood to exercise their ministry (e.g., Deuteronomy 18.5), so did the early Christian congregations. The growing recovery today of the idea of the common priesthood of all Christians may lead more churches to adopt a standing posture for the great prayer of thanksgiving at the heart of the Communion service.

DISCUSSION

For which parts of the Communion service do you usually stand, sit or kneel? How does your posture affect the way you think about God?

MOVEMENT

Movement is another way in which the body may be used in worship. A significant metaphor for the Christian understanding of life is that of a journey or pilgrimage, so processions and other movement within the liturgy can be seen as a physical symbol of that spiritual journey. On Palm Sunday, for example, a procession is often made into the church from another place, as the worshippers move with Jesus from the joy and excitement of his triumphal entry at the city gate into Jerusalem itself, the scene of his suffering and death. Walking with Jesus in a physical liturgical procession becomes a symbol of the Christian believer's desire and willingness to suffer in turn. (For more about seasonal processions see Session 3, especially the sections on The Presentation of Christ in the Temple and Maundy Thursday.)

Week by week in some churches processions are made within the Communion service. For the Gospel reading, a procession is formed which moves into the midst of the congregation, a sign of Christ the Word of God being sent by the Father into the world to redeem it. Later, when the table is prepared, members of the congregation may take up the bread and wine for the Communion and the collection that has been taken. That movement might be seen as symbolizing the offering of the lives of the worshippers to God.

Within the structure of several of the *Common Worship* services, specific provision is made for movement from one part of the church to another, because of the symbolic associations of the different parts of the building. For example, because the font is the place of baptism, a procession may be made to it by all those who are renewing their baptismal vows in some way, whether individuals to be confirmed or about to affirm their baptismal faith (see Session 7), or the whole congregation at the Easter Liturgy (see Session 3). This public liturgical use of the font might encourage worshippers to use it more privately at other times, perhaps by using the water in it to make the sign of the cross as a reminder of their baptism.

Similarly, because the front of the nave is the place where promises are usually made, e.g., by a bride and groom on their wedding day, or by candidates for confirmation, or by a priest about to be licensed by the bishop, it is also the place where the Decision is made by candidates for Initiation before processing to the font.

DISCUSSION

How often do you use movement within your church services? Who moves, and where and why do they move?

session 5 – HANDOUT

HYMNS		SONGS	
• sung *about* God?	• lasting	• sung *to* God?	• 'of the moment'
• doctrinal and cerebral	• classical-music roots	• emotive – little theological content	• Black Gospel / jazz / rock roots
• several verses – logical progression	• harmony-driven	• one simple theme – often repeated	• rhythm-driven assumes improvisation
	• assumes organ		

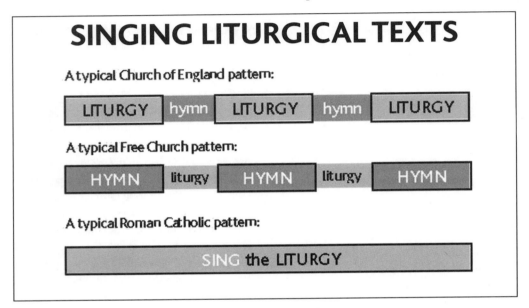

Intercessions for closing worship

For the Church universal, of which our church buildings are a visible symbol,
Lord, receive our thanks and prayer.
For our congregation as we remember your promise to be in the midst of your people when they worship,
Lord, receive our thanks and prayer.
For a place of prayer where we can be still and know that you are God.
Lord, receive our thanks and prayer.
For your blessings in the past and for a vision of the future,
Lord, receive our thanks and prayer.
For the gift of the Holy Spirit and new life in baptism,.
Lord, receive our thanks and prayer.
For the pardon of our sins when we fall short of your glory,
Lord, receive our thanks and prayer.

For a foretaste of your eternal kingdom in the sacrament of Holy Communion,
Lord, receive our thanks and prayer.
For the blessing of our vows and the crowning of our years with your goodness,
Lord, receive our thanks and prayer.
For the faith of those who have gone before us and for grace to persevere like them,
Lord, receive our thanks and prayer.
O God, from living and chosen stones
you prepare an everlasting dwelling place for your majesty.
Grant that in the power of your Holy Spirit
those who serve you in your Church on earth
may always be kept within your presence.
This we pray through Jesus Christ our Lord. **Amen.**

Before the next session

If you were determining a basic checklist of elements to include in a Sunday service that was *not* a Holy Communion, what would you include? Make it a list in two columns, one giving 'elements' of worship (for instance, things like 'a confession', 'a creed', 'the Lord's Prayer', 'the notices', 'hymns or songs') and one giving 'aspects' of worship (such as 'adoration', 'praise', etc.).]

1 A BASILICA

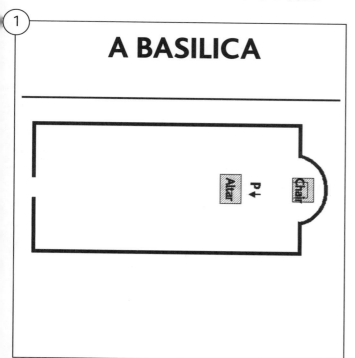

2 A MEDIEVAL PARISH CHURCH

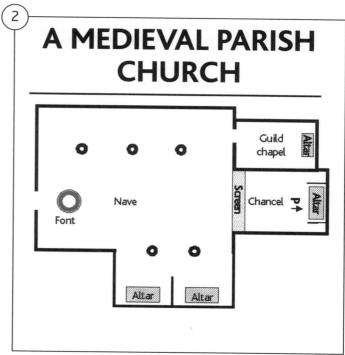

3 A PARISH CHURCH AT THE REFORMATION

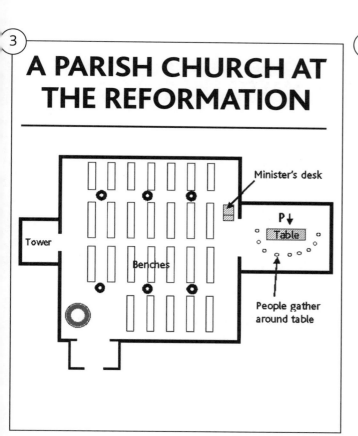

4 A MODERN PARSH CHURCH

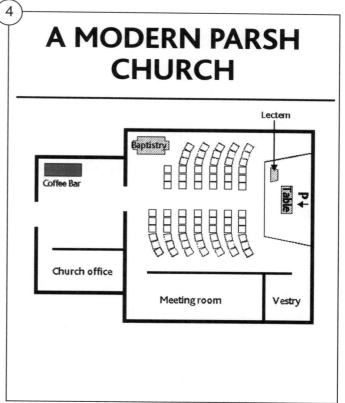

A SERVICE OF THE WORD

PART A – GETTING STARTED

Aim

To explore the history and content of non-eucharistic worship on Sundays, with particular emphasis on 'A Service of the Word'.

Leader's preparation

Have a good look through *Patterns for Worship*. Note especially pages 1–29 (Introduction and the text of A Service of the Word) and 191–242 (The Commentary). Have a look also at A Service of the Word in *Common Worship*, and at the services of Morning and Evening Prayer for Sundays and the resource materials provided (confessions, affirmations of faith, etc.).

Opening worship

Use material from either the traditional language (that is, Prayer Book) or modern language forms of Evening Prayer contained in the main *Common Worship* service book (or use Morning Prayer if your group meets during the day).

Session starter

As a rule, do you prefer Holy Communion services or non-eucharistic services (such as Morning or Evening Prayer or All-Age or 'Family' services)? Can you explain why?

PART B – HEART OF THE MATTER

See pages 52–5

PART C – TAKING IT FURTHER

For further discussion

Consider the following:

❖ Which aspects of your current Sunday services do you think would be most difficult for a visitor worshipping with you for the first time?

❖ Which of those aspects could be changed or improved?

❖ Is there a pattern of daily services at your church? Can you think of any ways of making people more aware of them, or of making them more accessible for more people (for instance, by changing the time, the form of service used, the venue, etc.)?

Reading and resources

Patterns for Worship (CHP, 1995) – contains the original authorized form of A Service of the Word, a huge amount of resource material, and excellent guidance on how to put a service together.

Trevor Lloyd, *A Service of the Word (Grove Worship Series No. 151)* (Grove Books, 1999) – a clear introduction to the history, use and possibilities of A Service of the Word.

T. Lloyd, J. Sinclair and M. Vasey, *Introducing Patterns for Worship (Grove Worship Series No. 111)* (Grove Books, 1990) – an introduction to the 'directory' approach to worship of *Patterns for Worship* and A Service of the Word.

Anne Barton, *All-Age Worship (Grove Worship Series No. 126)* (Grove Books, 1993) – advice for those planning All-Age or 'Family' services.

Closing worship

Use all or part of the service of Night Prayer from the *Common Worship* main service book (in either modern or traditional language).

Before the next session

Spend a little time making some notes about what your baptism means – *present* tense – to you today.

'... the minister ... may on occasions for which no provision is made in the Book of Common Prayer or by the General Synod ... use forms of service considered suitable by him [sic] for those occasions ...'

PART B – HEART OF THE MATTER

TWO SORTS OF WORSHIP

[VISUAL 1]

The first Christians seem to have had two main focuses for their worship:

❖ The fellowship meal (which later developed into what we would now call Holy Communion or the Eucharist);

❖ 'Word-based' worship involving Scripture and prayer.

'WORD-BASED' WORSHIP

This seems to have drawn from the worship pattern of the synagogue and the daily domestic prayer of every Jewish family. It included singing, the reading and exposition of Scripture, and the use of familiar prayers. We may perhaps see echoes of this sort of gathering in the references in Ephesians 5:18–20 ('psalms, hymns and spiritual songs') and 1 Corinthians 14:26:

'When you come together, each one has a hymn, a lesson, a revelation, a tongue, or an interpretation. Let all things be done for building up.'

In the history of Christian worship the 'Word-service' has manifested itself in three ways:

❖ As part of the pattern of daily prayer;

❖ As a 'stand-alone' service in the synagogue mould, focused on teaching and edification;

❖ As the first part of Holy Communion (sometimes called the 'ante-communion' or 'synaxis').

THE CHURCH OF ENGLAND'S DEVELOPING PATTERN

Archbishop Thomas Cranmer (1489–1556) produced two services, Morning and Evening Prayer, which he had simplified from the complex medieval monastic pattern (see diagram on handout). Cranmer wanted the people to attend Morning and Evening Prayer in the parish church with the parish priest every day. On Sunday morning he wanted them to come to Morning Prayer, Litany (a form of responsive prayer) and Holy Communion.

Cranmer's services were in English, rather than Latin, and parish clergy were under obligation to use Morning and Evening Prayer every day in the parish church, and to ring the bell beforehand so that all who wished to join the clergy could do so.

Though the clergy, in general, have stuck to the spirit (if not always the exact letter) of Cranmer's intention, the laity, on the whole, have not. Instead the Prayer Book services of Morning and Evening Prayer have become strongly associated with *Sunday* worship in the Church of England.

THE PRAYER BOOK PATTERN FOR MORNING AND EVENING PRAYER

The changes that Cranmer made to the medieval pattern were unique among the changes of the Reformation in Europe. The result is a clear pattern of hearing and responding that runs through each service (SEE VISUAL 2)

RECENT DEVELOPMENTS

Liturgical renewal over the last hundred years has brought several changes:

❖ Greater importance given to Holy Communion as the main act of worship on a Sunday;

❖ The consequent decline in Morning Prayer as a main Sunday service;

❖ A rediscovery of the corporate nature of prayer, and of the importance of daily prayer during the week, if not by the gathering of all the people in one place, then by the use of common patterns and forms of prayer by individuals or small groups in their different places.

CHANGING PATTERNS OF SUNDAY WORSHIP

Holy Communion has become much more common as the main act of worship on a Sunday, but it is not necessarily the most accessible service for newcomers: it includes many things that visitors sometimes find awkward, unfamiliar or hard to understand, such as the sharing of the Peace and going forward to receive Communion. By its very nature the Communion service can be seen as exclusive, as only those baptized and confirmed (or of communicant status in another Christian denomination) can take part in the main climax of the service, the reception of the consecrated bread and wine. Though a blessing is often offered, this is quite clearly a second-class option, even though it may be welcomed as better than nothing.

The result is a perceived need in some churches for something other than Holy Communion as a main service on Sundays. But what are the alternatives? In most situations Prayer Book Morning Prayer is not the answer.

In the 1960s many parishes began the search for something that was non-eucharistic, easy for outsiders to join in with, and not necessarily in Prayer Book language. This was not a new problem. In the nineteenth century many churches experimented with mission services and the so-called 'Third Service'. The latter was a service in addition to the statutory services of Morning Prayer (often combined with the Litany and Communion) and Evening Prayer. At first a 'Third Service' had to contain nothing other than hymns, anthems and material from the Bible and the Prayer Book.

In 1892 this was relaxed to allow material 'substantially in agreement with' the Bible and Prayer Book.

However, different people perceived these extra services in different ways. Some saw them as a 'bridge', which would help those on the fringe of the Church ultimately to find their way into Holy Communion and Morning and Evening Prayer. Others saw them as an important third strand for everybody, in addition to the Eucharist and the Daily Office pattern.

'FAMILY' AND 'ALL–AGE' SERVICES

One twentieth-century solution to the problem of accessibility for those on the fringe of the Church, or right outside it, was the 'Family' or 'All-Age' service. From the 1960s onwards many churches developed these services, as regular weekly acts of worship or as a once a month alternative to Holy Communion. There was no official provision: every parish priest used the flexibility permitted in the Canons. As long as Morning and Evening Prayer and Holy Communion were also offered in the same parish church on a Sunday, it was quite legal to devise an extra service provided that Canon B 5 was adhered to:

' . . . the minister . . . may on occasions for which no provision is made in the Book of Common Prayer or by the General Synod . . . use forms of service considered suitable by him [sic] for those occasions . . . '

'All variations in forms of service and all forms of service used under this Canon shall be reverent and seemly and shall be neither contrary to, nor indicative of any departure from, the doctrine of the Church of England in any essential matter'.

Standard forms were produced (for instance, in 1968, by the Church Pastoral Aid Society), but these were neither compulsory nor authorized.

There was at the same time a new vision of the place of children within the Church, which saw them as not merely the Church of tomorrow, but very much part of the Church of today. The report *Children in the Way* (NS/CHP 1988) called on the Liturgical Commission to devise services that would be suitable for all ages.

OTHER NEEDS

The success of these services and the need they seemed to meet sparked some fresh thinking about provision for non-eucharistic Sunday worship. In some churches, of course, the main need is not for something that is informal and for all ages, but for something more formal, with Sunday School groups (or their equivalent) for the children.

The ASB services of Morning and Evening Prayer mainly updated the language of the Prayer Book services and simplified the structure, but never really captured the imagination of the Church of England (though some churches used ASB Evening Prayer regularly).

The report *Faith in the City* (1985) highlighted the need for fresh resources to meet the needs of the inner cities and outer urban estates.

A SERVICE WITHOUT WORDS

The response to all these different needs was to conceive a new approach to Church of England liturgy – the 'directory' approach, which provided outlines and structures and lots of choices and resources, but did not specify the exact order of the elements or the particular texts to be used. In 1993 the Church of England authorized just such a thing – a service without any texts. It was called 'A Service of the Word' and was basically an outline of the key elements that ought to be included in a non-eucharistic Sunday service. It was like a skeleton waiting to be given some flesh.

In many ways A Service of the Word can be seen as the paradigmatic *Common Worship* service. It introduced the principle of a basic framework with considerable flexibility over content, combining local responsibility for worship with the need to preserve a sense of catholicity, commonality and orthodoxy.

WORSHIP IN MISSION MODE

In A Service of the Word, the Church of England is acknowledging that there is a need for worship to be flexible and adaptable to the particular needs of each congregation. In a culture which no longer shares Christian assumptions and in which practising Christians are a minority it is much more obvious that the Church is in the business of mission – sharing the good news of Jesus and calling others to worship the triune God. The most appropriate way of doing that will be determined in each local situation by the worshipping community, not by the Church of England's Liturgical Commission or the General Synod.

DISCUSSION

❖ If you have a regular non-eucharistic Sunday service as part of your pattern of services, do you see it as a 'bridge' to help people into other sorts of worship, or as a valuable act of worship in its own right? In your view, does it do its job?

❖ What are the positive and negative things, in your view, about 'All-Age' or 'Family' services?

DISCUSSION

Compare the list of elements from A Service of the Word (given on the handout) with the lists you prepared before the session. Are there any glaring contrasts between the two?

PATTERNS FOR WORSHIP

A Service of the Word first appeared in 1989 in a report by the Liturgical Commission called *Patterns for Worship*. This was not a book of services, but a guidebook – a directory and a resource book for producing non-eucharistic Church of England services. It provided plenty of flesh to put on the skeleton of A Service of the Word and included some sample services which showed different ways of putting a service together using different structures and lots of resources. *Patterns for Worship* was published in an amended authorized form in 1995.

GETTING THE BALANCE RIGHT

Patterns for Worship suggests that within a service there should be a balance between four main sorts of material (SEE VISUAL 3):

❖ Word

❖ Prayer

❖ Praise

❖ Action

Within these four categories, some elements are explicitly mentioned within the outline of A Service of the Word, and others are left to local decision.

DISCUSSION

❖ Look at the four main ingredients mentioned above. Which do you think are dominant in your church's worship, and at which are you weakest?

❖ If you look at the balance of these ingredients in your services, is there a difference between your Word-based services and your Holy Communion services?

A NEW WAY OF THINKING ABOUT WORSHIP

A look at the proportion of space given to different parts of *Patterns for Worship* shows how revolutionary it was:

❖ **A Service of the Word** itself (i.e. the outline) – 1 page

❖ **Notes** to A Service of the Word – 6 pages

❖ **Instructions and guidelines** for A Service of the Word – 10 pages

❖ **Resource sections** (including confessions, affirmations of faith, forms of intercession, forms of praise, greetings, blessings and endings, introductions for the Peace, etc.) – 145 pages

❖ **Sample services** – 84 pages

❖ **Commentary** (including advice on how to put a service together) – 52 pages

Though A Service of the Word only takes up one page, it is the most important part of the whole book and marked the beginning of a new way of thinking about worship in the Church of England.

A SERVICE OF THE WORD IN *COMMON WORSHIP*

The main *Common Worship* service book includes the basic outline of A Service of the Word. This is followed by both Prayer Book and modern language versions of Morning and Evening Prayer for use on Sundays, and two forms of Night Prayer. These are effectively outworkings of A Service of the Word. The *Common Worship* version of A Service of the Word also covers *daily* non-eucharistic services as well as Sunday worship. This makes the use of, for instance, *Celebrating Common Prayer* (CCP) for daily prayer, another outworking of A Service of the Word.

However, there is no attempt to give sample 'Family' or 'All-Age' services (lest it should stifle the creativity of local congregations). More examples of how to use A Service of the Word in these sorts of situations are expected in a new edition of *Patterns for Worship*.

As the above shows, *A Service of the Word* can be used in different contexts and to provide the framework for all sorts of different services. (See Visual 4) It brought the 'All-Age' service within the orbit of 'official' Church of England services, but can also work as a framework for other non-eucharistic morning services where children still go out to their own groups for learning. In addition, it can be used as the basis for an evening service (either formal or more informal), for 'Youth Services', so-called 'alternative worship' and for one-off and other 'special' sorts of service. When combined with parts of the Holy Communion services it can form the Gathering and the Liturgy of the Word for a eucharistic service (see Session 8).

ELEMENTS OF A SERVICE AND THE IMPORTANCE OF STRUCTURE

A Service of the Word is essentially a list of elements to be included in a non-eucharistic Sunday service in the Church of England. (Look again at the table on the Handout, and talk through it.) The focus is on the structure of the service, rather than on the detail of the content (though, clearly that is important too). This means giving attention to the key elements of a service and the order in which they are arranged. This focus on shape and structure has affected every area of liturgy and every part of the *Common Worship* series of services.

However, A Service of the Word does not lay down any particular shape or structure. *Patterns for Worship*, for instance, offers two possible ways of structuring a service:

❖ A 'block' structure – *Patterns for Worship*, page 23 (similar to that shown on the handout);

❖ A 'conversation' structure – *Patterns for Worship*, page 24 (which consists of several 'word' elements, each of which has an element of response). So, for example, a Scripture sentence is followed by a hymn of praise; an invitation is followed by the confession; and so on. (Compare this with Cranmer's approach – see Visual 2.)

Other ways of structuring services are possible and, indeed, encouraged – the key thing being that there *is* a clear structure and that this has been given some thought so that there is integrity between the content of the service and the way it is structured.

UNDERSTANDING THE LIMITS AND THE SCOPE

Whichever way the service is structured, A Service of the Word gives different levels of importance to different elements of the service:

❖ Some of the elements are **compulsory** (such as a confession and absolution, and the use of the Lord's Prayer).

❖ Some of the elements are **recommended** but not compulsory (such as the use of canticles or a set of responses).

❖ Other elements may be **added** at the discretion of the local leaders (such as hymns or songs).

There are also differences in the amount of choice allowed for each element:

❖ Some elements give **limited scope** (for instance, there are only a certain number of authorized confessions and absolutions). These tend to be things which can be doctrinally sensitive or controversial in Church of England understanding.

❖ Some of the elements give a **wide scope**, going well beyond the contents of the resource section of *Patterns for Worship* itself (for instance, the form of intercession used). The only constraint is that which applies to all services, that they should be appropriate for public worship and consistent with Church of England doctrine.

The notes to the service encourage the use of silence during the service and suggest points at which this may be particularly appropriate: at the beginning of the service, after the readings and the sermon, and during the prayers. The notes also make clear that the use of songs or hymns at various points in the service is a matter for local decision.

(Look again at the table on the handout and see the different combinations of level of importance and amount of scope.)

 DISCUSSION

Do you agree with the way that the elements of the service have been designated for level of importance and breadth of choice? If not, what changes would you make?

SESSION 6 – HANDOUT

The services of the medieval monastic pattern		Cranmer's pattern for the Church of England
12 midnight	Mattins	⎫
1 am	Lauds	⎬ Morning Prayer
7 am	Prime	⎭
9 am	Terce	
12 noon	Sext	
3 pm	None	
5 pm	Vespers	⎫ Evening Prayer
7 pm	Compline	⎭

The outline of *A Service of the Word*

Section	Scope	Element
Preparation	Compulsory, but unlimited	Greeting ◄
	Compulsory & limited choice	Authorized Prayers of Penitence
	Optional & unlimited	*Venite, Gloria, Kyries*, a hymn, song or set of responses may be used
	Compulsory but unlimited	The Collect ◄
Word	Compulsory & limited in part of year	Readings from Holy Scripture (two, or at the very least, one)
	Compulsory but unlimited	Psalm (or psalm-based hymn or song) or scriptural song
	Compulsory, but wide scope	Sermon ◄
	Compulsory & limited choice	Authorized creed or affirmation of faith
Prayers	Compulsory but unlimited	Intercessions and thanksgivings ◄
	Compulsory	The Lord's Prayer
Conclusion	Compulsory but unlimited	Clear ending – the grace, a blessing, a dismissal or other liturgical ending

> The service should have a clear 'liturgical' beginning, including a greeting between minister and people that establishes the gathered community of worshippers. Other elements such as sentences, singing, prayer and so on may also be part of the beginning of the service.

> The use of a Collect-style prayer is important but, unless the service is a Eucharist, this need not be the Collect of the day.

> The sermon need not be in a traditional form – the exploration of the scriptures could take the form of discussion or dialogue and might involve, for instance, drama or other creative art

> Thanksgiving could include music and singing as well as spoken words. If the Service of the Word forms the first part of a Communion service, then the element of thanksgiving would be covered by the Eucharistic Prayer.

Before the next session

Spend a little time making some notes about what your baptism means – *present* tense – to you today.

session 6 – **VISUALS**

1. TWO SORTS OF WORSHIP

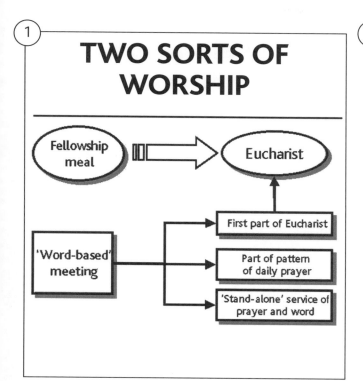

2. BCP MORNING AND EVENING PRAYER

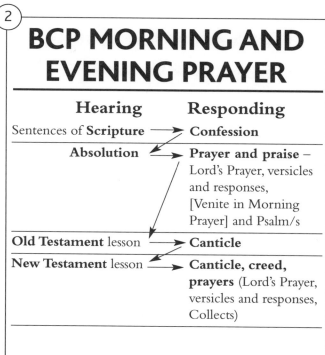

Hearing	Responding
Sentences of **Scripture** ⟶	**Confession**
Absolution ⟶	**Prayer and praise** – Lord's Prayer, versicles and responses, [Venite in Morning Prayer] and Psalm/s
Old Testament lesson ⟶	**Canticle**
New Testament lesson ⟶	**Canticle, creed, prayers** (Lord's Prayer, versicles and responses, Collects)

3. BALANCED WORSHIP

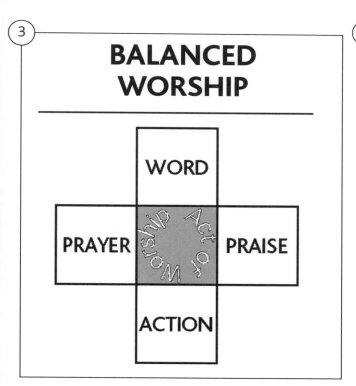

4. THE 'SERVICE OF THE WORD' UMBRELLA

INITIATION

PART A – **GETTING STARTED**

Aim

To explore the meaning and practice of initiation in the life and worship of the Church, and to look especially at the new provisions in *Common Worship*.

Leader's preparation

Read through the *Common Worship* service of: 'The Eucharist with Baptism and Confirmation together with Affirmation of Baptismal Faith and Reception into the Communion of the Church of England' (in *Common Worship: Initiation Services*) and the notes that follow. Perhaps focus especially on the less familiar aspects. Also read the 'Seasonal Material' (Appendix 2 to the material for Holy Baptism.) You will need to have copies of some of these texts, for example, the prayers over the water, available for group discussion during the session. For the Closing Worship, you will need to provide an appropriate basin and water (as an alternative to the font).

Opening worship

Sing or say a hymn or song invoking the Holy Spirit, for example: 'Come, Holy Ghost our souls inspire' (Bishop J. Cosin) or 'Spirit of the Living God, fall afresh on me' (Michael Iverson). Conclude with an appropriate prayer, such as the *Common Worship* Collect for the Second Sunday of Epiphany.

Session starter

Collect, perhaps on flipchart or OHP, and without too much discussion, members' responses to the question: 'What does your baptism mean to you today?'

PART B – **HEART OF THE MATTER**

See pages 60–3

PART C – **TAKING IT FURTHER**

For further discussion

[VISUAL 4 – THEOLOGICAL FRAMEWORK FOR BAPTISM]

In what sense does baptism involve separation from the world?

Those who are baptized are received into the Church, which is a universal community centred on God. How can local churches, including our own, better enable all God's children, of whatever age, to grow into the fullness of the pattern of Christ?

In what sense is the Church a community whose mission is serving God in redeeming the world?

Reading and resources

Book of Common Prayer – Baptism and Confirmation Services.

Common Worship: Initiation Services (Church House Publishing, 1998). The text of all the services, with a helpful introduction and concluding commentary that addresses some of the most frequently asked questions.

Mark Earey, *Initiation Services Training Pack* (*Praxis*, 1998). A helpful pack of materials for those wanting to explain *Common Worship – Initiation Services* to others. There are background notes, OHP master sheets, small group materials, and all with permission to photocopy for local use.

Colin Buchanan and Michael Vasey, *New Initiation Rites: a Commentary* (Grove Books 1998). A brief but comprehensive introduction to the *Common Worship* services.

Gilly Myers, *Using Common Worship: Initiation* Church House Publishing/*Praxis*, 2000. A practical guide for local churches written to help ministers, worship leaders and all involved with initiation ministry make the most of the possibilities afforded by the *Common Worship* initiation services and prayers.

On the Way: Towards an Integrated Approach to Christian Initiation – GSMisc. 444. (Church House Publishing, 1995). Key background thinking about the place of initiation in the process of evangelism and nurture.

Video
Welcome to Baptism: Journey of a Lifetime (Grayswood Studios, 1999). A 22-minute video for parents, godparents and all who bring young children for baptism. It is based on the *Common Worship* Baptism Service.

Closing worship
Use the 'Thanksgiving for Baptism' material linked with the *Common Worship* Orders for Morning and Evening Prayer on Sundays (p. 48 in the main *Common Worship* book).

Before the next session
These two questions will be used as a basis for group discussion at the beginning of Session 8 – Holy Communion 1.

1. Think back to your early experiences of the Communion service. Was there anything about it that you found difficult to understand?

2. Describe one particular Communion service that you found especially moving or helpful. What was it about the service that you particularly appreciated?

a journey
of a lifetime

PART B – HEART OF THE MATTER

INITIATION AND OUR CHRISTIAN IDENTITY

Most members of the Church of England will probably have been baptized as infants or young children, and confirmed as teenagers or young adults. From this perspective baptism and confirmation have been seen as related events, with baptism marking the beginning of the Christian life, and confirmation as the moment when individuals, who were baptized as children, made their own commitment to Christian faith and life.

In 1980 the *Alternative Service Book* challenged congregations brought up on the *Book of Common Prayer* with new services that seemed to approach baptism and confirmation differently. In the ASB, baptism, confirmation and Holy Communion was stressed as a unity. The baptism service for children was seen as deriving from this main service. Twenty years later the *Common Worship* services showed further development. There was a new overall title of 'Initiation Services'. The primary service was 'Holy Baptism', set out so that it could be used for both adult and infant candidates.

[Visual 2 – Baptism-focused Initiation]
In *Common Worship* baptism is seen as the primary initiation service; it begins a lifelong process by which we appropriate and enter into that initiation through other rites, which are primarily pastoral in nature. Two new post–initiation services, in addition to confirmation, meet particular pastoral needs: Affirmation of Baptismal Faith, and Reception into the Communion of the Church of England.

The *Common Worship* service, 'Thanksgiving for the Gift of a Child,' is also not an initiation service. It is one of a group of pastoral services and prayers that can be seen as surrounding and supporting initiation. It is included in the book of *Common Worship: Pastoral Services*.

THE HISTORY OF BAPTISM AND CONFIRMATION

The early years

The story of Christian initiation goes back to the earliest days of the Church. By the time that the New Testament came to be written, baptism was already established as the Church's initiation service. The few scriptural clues indicate that water was always used, that baptism was associated with the giving of the Holy Spirit, and that the Church generally baptized adults and whole families.

As the years passed, the increasing numbers of local congregations evolved their own baptismal practices. In third-century Rome, for example, candidates for baptism, 'catechumens', underwent a demanding three-year period of preparation. They were instructed in the Christian faith and taught to pray. In the days before their baptism they fasted and were exorcized. Baptisms took place during the Easter Vigil: children first, then men and women. After immersion in water, the newly baptized were anointed with the 'oil of thanksgiving' and admitted to the community prayers and Eucharist. Their instruction in the Christian faith continued after their baptism.

 DISCUSSION
How does the practice of the early Christians compare with your own experience of baptism and confirmation?

By the end of the fourth century, Christianity was the established religion of the Roman Empire. The once varied local patterns of initiation had become much more homogeneous. Easter remained the preferred time for baptism, though the period for instruction and preparation was much shorter. Candidates' names were recorded at the beginning of Lent, so there were just six weeks of preparation before baptism.

 DISCUSSION
Baptism is not so established a social custom as it used to be.
What are the implications for the Church's baptismal practice today?

Baptism in the Middle Ages

By the eighth century, Christianity had spread all over the Roman Empire and had become the dominant religion. Most baptisms were infant baptisms. Lent remained the main preparation period for adult candidates, with baptism at Easter. The bishop still presided over initiation services, and everyone, including the children, was baptized, received the laying on of hands and the Eucharist. (The latter, for infants, meant receiving a drop of consecrated wine from the bishop's or priest's finger.)

In the latter part of the Middle Ages, baptisms normally took place throughout the year and not just at Easter. Most infants would have been baptized within a week or so of birth. There was no longer any catechumenate or period of preparation for baptism. The ceremonies associated with the catechumenate, however, did not immediately disappear. Rather they were telescoped into one (normally infant) initiation service. The admission into the catechumenate was followed immediately by baptism and, if the bishop was there, confirmation.

In that sense, at the end of the Middle Ages, it was still just possible to feel the primitive unity of the initiation process in most parts of the Western Church. In England the most commonly used set of services was the Sarum Rite. These were the patterns of worship within which Thomas Cranmer and his reforming colleagues had grown up.

The first part of the Sarum service was 'the admission of catechumens'. It took place at the church door. It included naming, an initial signing with the cross, prayers of exorcism, and a further signing. The Gospel was read, the godparents and others present were required to say the Our Father, Hail Mary and the Creed. They were also instructed to teach the child these three texts as s/he grew up. Then the infant was taken into church and to the font for baptism. There the infant candidate was required, through his godparents, to renounce the works of Satan and profess the Christian faith. The child was then baptized in the name of the Holy Trinity, anointed, clad in his 'chrismal robe' and given a burning candle.

> *N*, receive a lamp burning and without fault: guard thy baptism: keep the commandments, so that when the Lord comes to the wedding thou mayest meet him together with the saints in the heavenly hall, that thou mayest have eternal life, and live for ever and ever. Amen

If a bishop was present, confirmation and Communion followed immediately. If not, these were delayed.

The Reformation era

The Reformation brought change to the English customs of baptism and confirmation. The services were simplified and some of the theological emphases altered.

Most of the changes during the Reformation years related to the various symbolic acts. These were on the whole mistrusted, and so were replaced by exhortation and prayer.

Exorcism

The lengthy medieval prayers of exorcism were first reduced and then omitted altogether.

Godparents

Cranmer retained the proxy speaking of the Sarum service – 'these infants must also faithfully for their part promise by you that be their sureties' – but increased the emphasis on the responsibility of the godparents to teach their godchildren the Christian faith.

Signing with the cross

Cranmer reduced the number of signings with the cross to just the one, and moved that away from before the baptism (where it had been linked with exorcism) to after the baptism where it was seen as a sign of reception into the Church.

Anointing

In the Sarum Rite anointing followed the triple renunciation ('holy oil'), the baptism and the confirmation (chrism). In Cranmer's first *Prayer Book* the infant was anointed once on the head after putting on the baptismal robe, 'the unction of his Holy Spirit'. In the later revisions anointing was omitted altogether.

Blessing of the font

Cranmer's first revision of the medieval baptism service in 1549 retained one prayer sanctifying the water in the font. In 1552 however, that prayer was revised. To avoid the idea of blessing things

rather than people, the next text prayed for 'all thy servants which shall be baptized in this water'. A further revision in 1662 prayed: 'sanctify this water to the mystical washing away of sin'.

Confirmation

As confirmation became separated from baptism the understanding of its meaning changed. Before the Reformation it was seen as God bestowing an additional gift of grace, strengthening ('confirming') and equipping the Christian for the battles of life. In Reformation times, however, confirmation was understood as the maturing child's own confirmation or ratification of their Christian faith in the presence of the bishop.

Baptism for 'those of riper years'

The 1662 Book introduced this additional initiation service to provide a service of baptism for all those who had been unable to be baptized during the time of England's civil war and Commonwealth.

 DISCUSSION
An increasing number of adults today are presenting themselves for initiation, both baptism and confirmation. Explore the textual differences in the service when adults are being baptized. If you have not yet experienced adult baptisms, discuss something of how you think adult candidates for initiation might understand the experience of baptism. Can you think of specific ways in which we might present this part of the service in order to make it as significant as possible for them?

Initiation in the Church of England in the twentieth century

The *Book of Common Prayer* served the worship needs of the Church of England until the twentieth century. In the latter half of the twentieth century, however, scholars began to question its theological assumptions about baptism.

Dom Gregory Dix, in 1946, described confirmation as the sacrament conveying the Holy Spirit. Geoffrey Lampe, in his book *The Seal of the Spirit* (1951) disagreed. He saw the fullness of initiation, including the gift of the Holy Spirit, as conveyed in baptism, so confirmation was unnecessary. In 1971 a General Synod report affirmed that 'sacramental initiation is complete in baptism', and made the case for admitting children to Holy Communion before confirmation.

Despite these recommendations, the *Alternative Service Book (1980)* retained the traditional place of confirmation. It did, however, present as primary the initiation service for people who were old enough to make their own decision of faith. This service was inspired by the practice of the early Church and incorporated baptism, confirmation and Holy Communion in one service. For infant baptisms the main text was adapted: confirmation and Holy

Communion were omitted, and other appropriate texts added.

In the ASB infant baptism service, questions of faith and belief were addressed to the parents and godparents, who had to answer both for themselves and for the child. This was a significant movement away from the 'proxy' response asked for in the BCP service. The service was briefer than the BCP service and the language was more accessible. The clear way in which the service highlighted symbolic actions proved particularly helpful. The signing with the cross, the baptism in water, the optional giving of the lighted candle and the 'welcome' into the church family were not only good teaching points: they also enabled people to understand the meaning of the sacrament at the level of their hearts as much as of their heads.

Those who wrote the ASB service hoped that the new emphasis would direct people away from seeing infant baptism as the norm and encourage them to take adult initiation more seriously. A new service, 'Thanksgiving for the Birth of/Adoption of a Child' was introduced as part of the initiation services, suggesting that it be used instead of, or at least before, infant baptism.

DISCUSSION
Some families, usually church families, choose to defer the baptism of their children until they are old enough to understand what is being promised. What are the advantages and disadvantages of this?

In the years following the publication of the ASB, the case for understanding baptism to be the 'complete' sacrament of initiation continued to be pressed. In 1991, Anglican liturgists from around the world met at Toronto to discusss initiation. Their Toronto statement 'Walk in Newness of Life' said: 'confirmation has a continuing pastoral role in the renewal of faith among the baptized but is in no way to be seen as a completion of baptism or as necessary for admission to communion'. Also in 1991, the Church of England General Synod commissioned a report on nurture in the faith and the catechumenate as well as new initiation services. The resulting report, *On the Way*, was published in 1995. In March 1997 the House of Bishops published guidelines to enable children in some parishes, provided there were suitable patterns of nurture and support, to receive Holy Communion before being confirmed. The new *Common Worship* Initiation Services were authorized in 1998.

While the *Common Worship* services stopped short of the complete Toronto 'vision', they did move the Church of England a little further in the direction it urged. The new initiation services, for example, responded to the Toronto encouragement of the catechumenal process, and its stress on making liturgical provision for the many ways in which people come to faith. The post-initiation rites offer different possibilities for candidates' differing needs (see Visual 1 – Patterns of Christian Initiation). The service of 'affirmation of baptismal faith', for example, can be used for baptized and confirmed Christians who, returning to church after a time of absence, wish to make a public affirmation of their baptism and confirmation.

Common Worship did not, however, wholly support the Toronto perception of confirmation as being in 'no way . . . necessary for admission to communion'. The authorized confirmation services 'follow carefully traditional Anglican practice and make no attempt to resolve these difficult questions'. (Commentary: *Common Worship Initiation Services*)

It is possible, though, that as the Church of England incorporates the new initiation services into its life and worship, the place of confirmation may gradually change. Arguably, the 1997 House of Bishops' guidelines as to the admission of children to Holy Communion before confirmation – under certain agreed conditions – have already begun that process.

DISCUSSION
The report *On the Way* amplifies five themes or concerns which have come to be focused on confirmation (See *On the Way*, pp.105–6):

❖ the acknowledgement of entry into adulthood, with all its dangers and responsibilities;

❖ the highlighting of individual faith, instructed, and professed before the Church;

❖ the need for a framework in order to follow up the results of a tradition of infant baptism;

❖ the importance of prayer and the gifts of the Spirit in initiation;

❖ responsible commitment to the life and mission of the local church.

Which of these would you normally associate with confirmation?
What do you feel about the other themes?

LOOKING AT THE
COMMON WORSHIP SERVICES
[VISUAL 2 – BAPTISM-FOCUSED INITIATION]

1. Stages in the journey of faith
The theological rationale for the *Common Worship* services is that baptism is the central event from which everything to do with Christian initiation flows. It is the first of many stages where growth and change can be perceived and named.

❖ **Holy Baptism** Christians are encouraged to see their baptism as a continuing reality throughout the whole of their lives, something which defines their identity as ever-maturing Christians. Baptism is about participation in the life of God and about sharing his mission to the world. It is not simply a one-off 'admission into the family' event.

❖ **Confirmation and Holy Communion** Confirmation with first Holy Communion is the traditional expression of the maturing faith of those who were baptized as infants and who wish to make the commitment of Christian faith for themselves. (The 1997 House of Bishops' guidelines on children and Holy Communion, however, have introduced the possibility of change to the traditional linking of confirmation with first Holy Communion.) Adults who have not been baptized as infants are normally baptized, confirmed and receive first Holy Communion in an initiation service that contains all these elements.

❖ **Affirmation of baptismal faith** [Visual 1 – Patterns of Christian initiation] The journey of faith has its ups and downs. Some people, for example, experience a 'tailing off' of faith after baptism and confirmation. This may, however, be followed by a renewed discovery of the meaning of the Christian faith and a desire to make a public statement of their return to faith and experience of grace. *Common Worship* gives an opportunity for the public affirmation of this return to faith. Part of the service takes place at the font, and candidates may optionally sign themselves with water or be sprinkled with it as a reminder of baptism. The service is careful to avoid any suggestion of a second baptism.

❖ **Reception into the communion of the Church of England** *Common Worship* also offers one further pastoral service: the public reception into the communicant life of the Church of England of those who have been episcopally confirmed in other Churches. This service does not include the laying on of hands, as happens at confirmation. Rather, the president 'takes the hand of each person to be received, saying '*N*, we recognize you as a member of the one, holy catholic and apostolic Church and we receive you into the communion of the Church of England'.

2. Times and seasons

One of the new insights given by the *Common Worship* initiation services comes from the move towards understanding baptism through additional images to the 'death and resurrection' ones. The new services contain seasonal texts that supplement the general texts printed in the main Holy Baptism service. There are three seasonal alternatives: Epiphany/Baptism of Christ/Trinity; Easter/Pentecost; and All Saints. Different texts are given for the Introduction, the Collect, the Prayer over the Water, the Peace, the Prayers of Intercession, the Prayer after Communion and the Blessing.

The 'Epiphany/Baptism of Christ/Trinity' texts, for example, emphasize the links between Jesus' baptism and the baptism of his followers. The imagery of baptism is linked with the imagery of revelation, restoration, transfiguration and inspiration. The 'All Saints' texts link baptism with the journey of faith made by all

Christian people and especially with the saints, and point the newly baptized to their future in Christ. The Easter/Pentecost texts emphasize the images of Christ's death and resurrection.

DISCUSSION
Some of the words of the baptism service may be varied, according to the season of the Church's year; for example, Epiphany, Easter, Trinity and All Saints.

Look at some of the seasonal alternatives (prayers over the water, for example) and discuss how the seasonal emphases point up different aspects of Christian life and hope.

3. Images and symbols
[VISUAL 3 – INITIATION – BIBLICAL IMAGES]

The New Testament writers used many images to describe what happened when someone became a Christian. Many of these are listed, with Bible references, in the commentary to the *Common Worship* services printed at the back of the book of Initiation Services (p. 191). The scriptural imagery includes liberation, new birth, new creation, reconciliation, justification, darkness to light, stripping and clothing, dying and rising, building.

DISCUSSION
Use the table of biblical references in the commentary at the back of the book of Initiation Services (p. 191) to explore the list of scriptural images.

Which images are new to you? How do they widen your understanding of the meaning of your baptism and confirmation?

Services are not 'all words'. The initiation services make use of various symbolic actions to convey the meaning of the sacrament. Some are essential and some optional. Symbolic actions special to the initiation services include: presentation of candidates; signing with the cross; the use of water; clothing with a white robe; anointing with oil; standing before the bishop; the imposition of the bishop's hand on each candidate; the giving of a lighted candle.

DISCUSSION
Which of these symbols speak most powerfully to you, and why?

Which of these are used at other church services? What do they symbolize then?

session 7 – HANDOUT

Two Thousand Years of Christian Initiation

	3rd c. Church	Medieval (Sarum)	Book of Common Prayer	Common Worship
WHO?	• Adults, families	• Mainly infants	• Mainly infants	• All ages, still mainly infants
PREPARATION?	• Adults: three years	• Adults: Lent • Infants: none, but post-baptism teaching later	• None: catechism later	• Adults: provision varies from parish to parish • Infants: none (but encouraged for their parents)
WHEN?	• At Easter	• Adults: at Easter • Infants: within a week of birth	• Sundays at any time of year	• Any time of year (seasonal material provided)
CONFIRMATION AND COMMUNION?	• At same time as baptism	• Later, if bishop not present at baptism	• Later	• Adults, at same time as baptism, or shortly after • infants, later

On the Way

The report *On the Way* amplifies five themes or concerns which have come to be focused on confirmation (See *On the Way*, pp.105–6):

- the acknowledgement of entry into adulthood, with all its dangers and responsibilities;

- the highlighting of individual faith, instructed, and professed before the Church;

- the need for a framework in order to follow up the results of a tradition of infant baptism;

- the importance of prayer and the gifts of the Spirit in initiation;

- responsible commitment to the life and mission of the local church.

Common Worship Initiation – Symbolic Actions

BAPTISM
presentation of candidates; signing with cross; use of water; optional clothing in white robe; optional anointing; Peace and welcome; giving of lighted candle

CONFIRMATION
standing before the bishop; imposition of bishop's hand; optional anointing

AFFIRMATION
optional sprinkling, or self-signing with water

RECEPTION
handshake

Before the next session

1. Think back to your early experiences of the Communion service. Was there any thing about it that you found difficult to understand?

2. Describe one particular Communion service that you found especially moving or helpful. What was it about the service that you particularly appreciated?

1 PATTERNS OF CHRISTIAN INITIATION

Baptized as child – no further church contact – returns to faith later

BAPTISM

Exploration
Commitment
CONFIRMATION
Growth & Nurture

Brought up with church – falls away in late teens – returns to faith in later life

BAPTISM
CONFIRMATION

Exploration
Commitment
AFFIRMATION
Growth & Nurture

2 BAPTISM-FOCUSED INITIATION

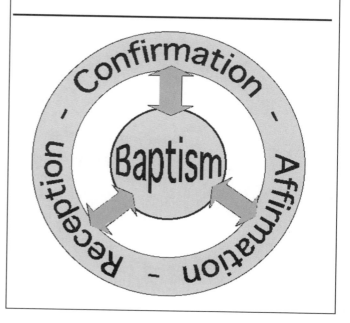

Confirmation – Affirmation – Reception – Baptism

3 INITIATION – BIBLICAL IMAGES

liberation
BU-IL-DI-NG
new birth
darkness to light
reconciliation
New Creation
stripping & clothing
stripping & clothing
illumination
recognition
dying & rising
cleansing

4 THEOLOGICAL FRAMEWORK FOR BAPTISM

- **SEPARATION**
  from life alienated from God

- **RECEPTION**
  into a universal community centred on God

- **TRANSFORMATION**
  to become more like Christ

- **MISSION**
  working with God in redeeming his world

HOLY COMMUNION 1

PART A – GETTING STARTED

Aim

To explore the shape and structure of the Holy Communion service.

Leader's preparation

Try to familiarize yourself with the Holy Communion services of *Common Worship: Services and Prayers for the Church of England*, including the alternative texts available and the notes which follow the rite.

It would be helpful for members of the group to have a copy of *Common Worship: Holy Communion Order One* during the session.

Opening worship

Sing a hymn or worship song about the death of Jesus.

Keep a time of quiet to reflect on the love of God revealed by the cross of Christ, and the way we have experienced that love in the Holy Communion service.

End the silence with the following prayer:

> Lord Jesus Christ,
> we thank you that in a wonderful sacrament
> you have given us the memorial of your passion:
> grant us so to reverence the sacred mysteries
> of your body and blood
> that we may know within ourselves
> and show forth in our lives
> the fruits of your redemption;
> for you are alive and reign
> now and for ever.
> **Amen.**

*Adapted from the Post-Communion
prayer for Maundy Thursday*

Session starter

In small groups, discuss your answers to the questions you were asked to think about in preparation for this session.

PART B – HEART OF THE MATTER

See pages 68–71

PART C – TAKING IT FURTHER

For further discussion

Which part of the Communion service do you like the best? Can you explain why?

Reading and resources

David Holeton (ed.), *Renewing the Anglican Eucharist – Findings of the Fifth International Anglican Liturgical Consultation* (Grove Worship Series No. 135) (Grove Books, 1996). A summary of the conference that laid down key principles for the structuring of the Communion service.

Mark Beach, *Using Common Worship: Holy Communion* (CHP/*Praxis*, 2000). A practical guide to the Communion service.

Jeremy Fletcher, *Common Worship Eucharistic Rites* (Grove Worship Series No. 159) (Grove Books, 2000). A readable introduction to the *Common Worship* Holy Communion service.

Gregory Dix, *The Shape of the Liturgy* (Dacre, 1945). An enormously influential classic which still demands serious attention, although liturgical scholarship has moved on considerably since it was written.

Pete Ward (ed.), *Mass Culture: Eucharist and Mission in a Post-Modern World* (BRF, 1999). A good source of thinking about the Holy Communion service from a variety of perspectives across the denominations.

Mark Earey, *Holy Communion Services Training Pack* (*Praxis*, 2000). Largely concerned with explaining the differences between *ASB* and *Common Worship*, but also good on demonstrating the structure of the rite.

Closing worship

Using the handout, and following the structure for intercessions suggested in *Common Worship: Holy Communion*, ask the group to pool their particular suggestions under each heading, then allocate one person to be responsible for leading some brief prayers under each heading. At the end, the group leader concludes the prayers using one of the Collects or Other Endings for Intercession from *Common Worship*.

Before the next session

Which of these names for the Holy Communion service do you prefer and why?

Holy Communion
The Eucharist
The Lord's Supper
The Breaking of Bread
The Liturgy
The Mass
The Holy Mysteries

PART B – HEART OF THE MATTER

THE HEART OF CHRISTIAN WORSHIP

In his first letter to the Church at Corinth, St Paul reminds the early Christians that

> 'on the night he was betrayed, Jesus took bread, and after giving thanks to God broke it and said:
>
> "This is my body, which is for you; do this in memory of me."
>
> In the same way, he took the cup after supper, and said:
>
> "This cup is the new covenant sealed by my blood. Whenever you drink it, do this in memory of me."
>
> For every time you eat this bread and drink this cup, you proclaim the death of the Lord, until he comes.'
>
> (1 Corinthians 11.23–6)

From that time until this, the Holy Communion service has been at the heart of Christian worship. Christians have broken bread and drunk wine in 'memory' of Jesus, in obedience to his command. In the next session we will look at the history of the service and see how Christians of many ages have tried to interpret it. In this session we look in detail at a modern service of Holy Communion (*Common Worship: Holy Communion Order One*) to see the overall structure of the service and how each part contributes to the total picture.

SERVING ONE ANOTHER – DIFFERENT ROLES IN THE HOLY COMMUNION SERVICE

One of the first words we encounter in the service order is the word **president**. This is the term used for the priest who leads the Holy Communion service, and it is a much better name than the older term **celebrant**, because it is the whole congregation gathered for worship that celebrates the service. The ministry of lay people is expressed through their active participation together in the words and actions of the service, as well as by members of the congregation reading the Scripture passages, leading the prayers of intercession and, after authorization, assisting with the distribution of Holy Communion. But within that ministry of the whole congregation there is a particular ministry exercised by the **president**, who in presiding over the whole service holds word and sacrament together and draws the congregation into a worshipping community. The president expresses this ministry at several key points of the service, by saying the Opening Greeting, the Absolution, the Collect, the Peace and the Blessing, as well as by leading the eucharistic prayer, breaking the consecrated bread and receiving the sacrament.

In some traditions the president is assisted by a **deacon**, who, among other functions, may read the Gospel, prepare the table and gifts, and dismiss the people. These are tasks that could be performed by a reader or other lay person, or by an assistant priest. This diaconal (deacon's) ministry is essentially a ministry of service, serving both the president and the people, and reminding the Christian community of its call to be a servant Church.

THE STRUCTURE OF THE SERVICE

The service has two main sections: **The Liturgy of the Word** and **The Liturgy of the Sacrament**. (See Visual 1.) The former is usually centred around the lectern or pulpit or both, and the latter around the 'holy table', sometimes called the 'altar'. One of the common features of many modern Holy Communion services is the desire to preserve a proper balance between **Word** and **Sacrament**, as the people of God meet first around the Bible to discover Christ's presence in his Word, and then around the table where his presence is focused in bread and wine.

These central sections are preceded by a shorter section called **The Gathering**, which helps the people of God to come together in praise and in penitence. After Communion comes a final section called **The Dismissal**. Although short, it is a very important part of the service, for in it the people of God are sent out from the worshipping community to serve God in his world.

'ALTAR' OR 'HOLY TABLE'

The official Church of England services speak of a ' holy table', but in ordinary use Anglicans often speak of the 'altar'. For some in the Church of England the question of which term is used carries with it considerable significance. For some people (mainly from the Catholic tradition) the use of the term 'altar' seems the most natural, as they see it as the place where the sacrifice of Christ upon the cross is remembered or, indeed, 'offered' in some way. Other Anglicans (mainly from the Evangelical tradition) are unhappy with this talk of altars and offering, because they want to emphasize the unrepeatable and all-sufficient sacrifice of Christ made 'once for all upon the cross'. The use of 'table' stresses for them that the Holy Communion is primarily a fellowship meal, the Lord's Supper, at which they recall a sacrifice, but one which was offered in another place at another time.

 DISCUSSION
'Altar' or 'holy table'. Which term do you prefer and why?

THE GATHERING

[USE VISUAL 2 THROUGHOUT THE REMAINDER OF THIS SESSION]

The Greeting

At the very beginning of the service the president greets the people. In some churches, the Greeting is preceded by:

In the name of the Father,
and of the Son,
and of the Holy Spirit. **Amen.**

This reminds the Christian community right at the beginning of the service that everything that is to take place within it is done in the name of God and to his glory. Sometimes these words may be accompanied with the making of the sign of the cross, as those present recall their baptism into Christ.
Then the president continues:

The Lord be with you
and also with you.

This greeting and response (or its alternatives)

❖ declares that the service has started as the people of Christ greet each other and remember that the Lord is with them;

❖ shows the relationship between the president, who takes the initiative in greeting the people, and the people, who recognize the president's authority to preside;

❖ enables the people to respond together and step forward into the service as a body rather than as a collection of individuals.

The Prayer of Preparation

Almighty God,
to whom all hearts are open . . .

emphasizes that we can only meet God in this service if he prepares us for that meeting, and part of that preparation comes through our penitence for our sins. This leads into the next section.

Prayers of Penitence

In these prayers the people confess that they have sinned against God (and, in the case of the first option, against their neighbour too). These prayers are deliberately very general in tone, suitable for use by the whole Christian community as it gathers for worship. (For more about individual and corporate penitence see Session 10.) The president then says **The Absolution**, reminding the people of the gracious forgiveness of God, and claiming that forgiveness for them as they move forward into their act of worship set free from their sins. In some churches (and in some parts of the Church's year) there may be a preference to put the Prayers of Penitence later in the service, as a response to the Liturgy of the Word.

Gloria in excelsis

This ancient hymn of praise begins with the song of the angels at Christ's birth, and goes on to reflect how it is the same Christ who is present today to hear our prayers and take away our sins.

Glory to God in the highest
and peace to his people on earth . . .
Lord Jesus Christ . . .
you take away the sin of the world:
have mercy on us;
you are seated on the right hand of the Father:
receive our prayer.

The Collect

[SEE VISUAL 3]

This prayer said by the president is, as its name suggests, designed to 'collect' up the prayers of the congregation. The president says 'Let us pray' or some more specific words, and then there is a period of silent prayer, in which the people can reflect upon the wonder of God and his graciousness in forgiving their sins, and prepare their minds and hearts to encounter him in Word and Sacrament. At the end of the silence, **The Collect** gathers all those private prayers together, as the community moves into the next section of the service.

 DISCUSSION
The Prayers of Penitence feature during the initial part of the service (the Gathering), although they may be transposed to a later point after the Liturgy of the Word. What do you think are the advantages and disadvantages of each position?

THE LITURGY OF THE WORD

Readings

The Liturgy of the Word begins with two or three readings from Scripture, together with a Psalm which follows the first reading. (For more about the use of the Bible in worship see Session 4.) The Psalm can be used in several ways: sung to traditional Anglican chant, read in alternate verses by reader and congregation, or read or sung as a Responsorial Psalm. In this case, the reader or singer performs a few verses at a time, and then the congregation responds by saying or singing a short phrase in response.

The Gospel

The readings culminate in the proclamation of the Gospel, the good news of Jesus. The people stand as a mark of respect for Christ's presence in the Gospel. In some churches the importance of the Gospel reading may be emphasized by a procession, by the use of candles and incense, or by reserving the reading of the Gospel to a deacon or a priest.

The Sermon

The readings are immediately followed by **The Sermon**, the main purpose of which is to expound the readings. The notes which accompany the service stipulate that, as the sermon is an integral part of the Liturgy of the Word, a sermon should be preached at all celebrations of Holy Communion, at least on all Sundays and principal Holy Days.

The Creed

This is usually the Nicene Creed, but on occasion another authorized creed or affirmation of faith may be used. Whereas in the readings and the sermon only one aspect of the Christian faith could be looked at in detail, now the whole framework of that faith is presented in outline. In our modern services this creed is presented in the plural form: **'We believe in one God . . .'** The members of the worshipping community together reaffirm the faith of the Church. This corporate expression of faith is not intended to play down the importance of the personal faith of each Christian believer but rather incorporates it within the faith of the Christian community. At baptism, candidates are asked as individuals whether they believe in God who is Father, Son and Holy Spirit, and when the members of the congregation are asked to declare their faith on that occasion, they do so as individuals, each recalling their own baptism. (See Session 7.) But at the Holy Communion service we celebrate our continuing membership within the Body of Christ by confessing our faith together, just as we have earlier confessed our sins together.

Prayers of Intercession

This section of the service is one where a considerable degree of flexibility is allowed, although the service order suggests topics which are usually to be included:

> The Church of Christ
> Creation, human society, the Sovereign and those in
> authority
> The local community
> Those who suffer
> The communion of saints

The notes accompanying the service suggest that this is another point where silence would be appropriate, as the prayer leader gives the congregation the opportunity to make the prayers their own. Lay people are encouraged to lead these prayers, and there are many resource books available to help those who are unfamiliar with this particular ministry. In some churches the prayers may be introduced by the president, who may also conclude them with an appropriate Collect, again gathering up the prayers and concerns of the congregation as the service moves into its next main section.

THE LITURGY OF THE SACRAMENT
The Peace

The people of God stand and affirm their identity as the Body of Christ. The president may introduce the peace with a suitable sentence, and then he or she greets the people. All may exchange a handshake or other sign of peace. This is a very ancient Christian practice. The 'kiss of peace' is referred to by St Paul in several of his epistles, while some of the orders of prayer from the earliest days of the Christian Church mention the exchange of the Peace.

In its position here, as the Liturgy of the Word moves into the Liturgy of the Sacrament, the Peace acts as a kind of hinge of the whole service. It reminds us of the words of Jesus in Matthew 5.23–4, where Jesus tells us to be reconciled to our brother before bringing our gift to the altar. Now, before the members of the congregation go forward to recognize Christ in the breaking of the bread, and receive the Body of Christ in their hands, they turn and recognize the Body of Christ in one another, and stretch out their hands to them too.

DISCUSSION

Sharing the Peace can be an emotive issue for some churchgoers. What do you think is gained by it, and what might be the objections to doing it?

Preparation of the table

The focus now moves to the holy table. The offerings of money for the needs of the Church and the world may be presented. At the same time, the president (or deacon/diaconal minister if there is one) prepares the bread and the wine, and in many churches pours a little water into the chalice to mix it with the wine, sometimes seen as a reminder of the blood and the water which flowed from the side of Jesus on the cross, or as a sign of the two natures of Christ. If incense is used, the president may cense the gifts of bread and wine and the holy table, before the president and the people are censed. Incense is a sign of prayers rising to God, as well as a symbol of God's presence in the midst of his people who gather together to worship him. (As the hymn 'We Three Kings' puts it: 'Incense owns a deity nigh'.) In some churches the president washes his hands as a sign of the purity demanded of all Christians as they approach the holy table.

[SEE VISUAL 4]
At the heart of the service, we remember the actions of Jesus at the Last Supper he shared with his friends: how he **took** bread and **blessed** it (i.e., gave thanks over it), **broke** it, and **gave** it to the disciples. So the president performs the same four actions over the bread and the wine at every Communion service.

❖ The president **takes** the bread and the wine into his or her hands, either while the table is being prepared, or during the Eucharistic Prayer which follows.

❖ The president leads the people in **giving thanks** over the bread and wine in **the Eucharistic (or Thanksgiving) Prayer**. (For a full discussion of the Eucharistic Prayer see Session 9). This prayer is immediately followed by **the Lord's Prayer**. The Lord's Prayer has usually been placed at this point in the service because of its petition 'give us today our daily bread' which a number of early theologians saw as referring to the bread of the Communion.

❖ The president **breaks** the consecrated bread. The breaking of bread began as a practical necessity in the early Church as the small loaves were divided into smaller pieces for the distribution. In time, Christians began to see various symbolic meanings in this action. One, derived from 1 Corinthians 10.17, is suggested by one of the texts provided for use at this point

> **Though we are many, we are one body, because we all share in one bread.**

The action of breaking bread from one loaf is a symbol of the unity of Christian people in Christ.

In later centuries, the breaking of the bread would be seen as symbolizing the death of Christ whose body was broken on the cross. This is an interpretation emphasized by the anthem **Agnus Dei** which may be used at this point:

> **Lamb of God, you take away the sin of the world: grant us peace.**

❖ The president **distributes** the consecrated elements. Before the actual distribution the president invites the people to draw near and receive the Body and Blood of Christ, and the people may respond in the words of the **Prayer of Humble Access** (or an alternative prayer):

> **We do not presume to come to this your table, merciful Lord . . .**

The Prayer of Humble Access is based on the prayer composed by Cranmer for the 1548 Order of Communion to help the people share in and prepare themselves for fuller participation in the Lord's Supper. It reminds us that we approach the Lord's table only because he is kind enough to invite us.

All is now ready, and the president and people receive the Communion. Various words are authorized for use at the distribution, but they all require the communicant to say **Amen** before receiving. 'Amen' is a Hebrew word meaning 'certainly' or 'assuredly'. It acknowledges that a saying is valid or binding. So the communicant's 'Amen' is an integral part of the act of Communion.

DISCUSSION

At what point in the service do you think the notices should be given out (if at all)? (The notes within *Common Worship* suggest before the preparation, before the prayers of intercession or before The Dismissal.)

Prayer after Communion

When the Communion is over, the service order states that silence is kept, as the president and people together observe a time to reflect on the wonder of Christ's love shown in the Communion service. The time of silence ends with prayers, usually one said by the president, and then a second prayer of thanksgiving said by all.

THE DISMISSAL

This section is deliberately brief, for having received Communion and said thank you, nothing remains but to go from the service to serve God in his world.

Blessing

The president may use a **blessing**, although this remains optional. There are some who think that a verbal blessing is superfluous after having received God's greatest blessing in Communion.

Words of dismissal

These may be said by the deacon, the servant minister who gives this commission to his fellow servants:

> Go in peace to love and serve the Lord.
> **In the name of Christ. Amen.**

or alternatively

> Go in the peace of Christ.
> **Thanks be to God.**

DISCUSSION

Does The Dismissal in your church feel like you are being sent out to serve God in the world?

session 8 – HANDOUT

Use this sheet to write down your own particular concerns under the five headings below, before pooling them within the group

The Church of Christ

Creation, human society, the Sovereign and those in authority

The local community

Those who suffer

The communion of saints

Before the next session

Which of these names for the Holy Communion service do you prefer and why?

Holy Communion   The Liturgy
The Eucharist   The Mass
The Lord's Supper   The Holy Mysteries
The Breaking of Bread

1

TWO SECTIONS OF HOLY COMMUNION

Word

Sacrament

2

HOLY COMMUNION ORDER ONE

Gathering	• Greeting – Prayer of Preparation – Penitence – Gloria – Collect
Liturgy of the Word	• Readings – Sermon – Creed – Intercessions
Liturgy of the Sacrament	• Peace – Preparation – Eucharistic Prayer – Lord's Prayer – Breaking of Bread – Humble Access – Distribution – Prayer after Communion
Dismissal	• Blessing – 'Go in peace...'

3

THE COLLECT

Invitation to pray (president)

Silent prayer (all)

Collect (president)

4

THE FOURFOLD EUCHARISTIC ACTION

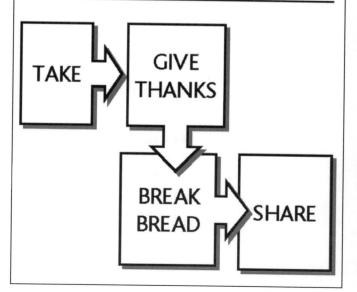

TAKE → GIVE THANKS → BREAK BREAD → SHARE

HOLY COMMUNION 2

PART A – GETTING STARTED

Aim
To explore some of the history and theology of the Holy Communion service and see how that history and theology is reflected in a modern Eucharistic Prayer.

Leader's preparation
Have a look through the Eucharistic Prayers of *Common Worship: Holy Communion Order One* in the light of the latter part of the Heart of the Matter section for this session concerning Prayer A. See if you can recognize the distinctive parts of the Eucharistic Prayer in Prayers B to H.

Opening worship
Read 1 Corinthians 11.23–25 and Mark 14.12–25

Keep a time of silence

Sing a hymn or worship song about Holy Communion.

Session starter
Which of these names for the Holy Communion service do you prefer and why? (See also Visual 1)

Holy Communion
The Eucharist
The Lord's Supper
The Breaking of Bread
The Liturgy
The Mass
The Holy Mysteries

PART B – HEART OF THE MATTER

See pages 76–9

PART C – TAKING IT FURTHER

For further discussion
If an alien from another planet (or from your parish!) was to ask what a Eucharistic Prayer is *for*, what would you say?

Which of the Eucharistic Prayers from *Common Worship* are used in your church? Which of them do you prefer and why?

Reading and resources

See reading and resources list for Session 8.

In addition:

Colin Buchanan and Charles Read, *The Eucharistic Prayers of Order One* (Grove Worship Series No. 158), (Grove Books, 2000). A full discussion of the background and theology of the prayers.

Closing worship

Use the Form of Preparation for Holy Communion (*Common Worship: Holy Communion*) as a way of preparing yourselves as individuals and as a group for the next service of Holy Communion that you attend.

> Come, Holy Ghost (said or sung as appropriate)
> The Exhortation
> The Commandments *or* The Summary of the Law *or*
>   The Comfortable Words *or* The Beatitudes
> Silence
> Confession
> Absolution (if led by a deacon or lay person *us* is substituted for *you*)

Before the next session

In Jesus Christ, God is 'overthrowing an order of life corrupted by sin and death and bringing to birth a renewed creation, a creation alive with the healing presence of God's Spirit'. (*Common Worship: Wholeness and Healing*: Theological Introduction).

In preparation for this session look up the following Bible references and see how they illustrate this perception of salvation:

> Luke 4.18–21;
> Luke 12:50
> John 9 (especially v. 3)
> Romans 3.21–26
> Romans 8.3–4, 18–30
> Colossians 1.15–27

PART B – HEART OF THE MATTER

ONE SERVICE – MANY NAMES

[SEE VISUAL 1]

The Holy Communion service is known by many other names – the Eucharist, the Lord's Supper, the Breaking of Bread, the Liturgy, the Mass, the Holy Mysteries, and so on. Each of these names tells us something about the service, and each Christian group has preferred one or other of these names, depending on what it has seen to be the most important aspect of the service, for the Holy Communion has undergone many changes during its history, both in the form of the service and also in what has been believed about it.

THE EARLY CENTURIES

[SEE VISUAL 2]

The title 'Eucharist' comes from the Greek *eucharistia*, meaning 'thanksgiving', which was used in New Testament times to translate the Hebrew *berakah*, meaning 'blessing'. Shortly before his death, Jesus shared a last supper with his disciples, and during it he offered praise and thanks to God in the Jewish manner usual on such occasions. According to the New Testament traditions (1 Corinthians 11.23–25 and Luke 22.14–20 seem to represent one tradition; Mark 14.22–25 and Matthew 26.26–29 another), Jesus gave thanks over the bread and wine and identified himself with the food that would be shared by his followers. 'This is my Body'. 'This is my Blood'. Jesus also told his followers to 'do this in memory of me', and so when the early Christians met for worship, they did just that – they shared bread and wine together to remember Jesus.

Scholars are more or less agreed that the earliest Christian eucharists were in fact complete meals shared together by the local Christian community where everyone brought some food along and shared it with the other believers. During this meal bread and wine would be taken as the believers remembered Christ and celebrated his presence with them, and gave thanks to God for what he had done for them through Christ. It is not clear whether the earliest Christians associated Christ's presence with the elements of bread and wine themselves, or with the action of blessing and sharing them. They also saw the meal as a foretaste of things to come, when God's kingdom would finally arrive in power and there would be a great banquet shared with Christ, a banquet to which he often referred in his teaching and which he anticipated in the miracles of feeding the multitudes.

It wasn't long before the early believers began to run into difficulties. In a Gentile environment where banquets in honour of the gods were common, the feasting, and sometimes the drunkenness, could overwhelm the special nature of what was being remembered. Paul, writing to the Christians in Corinth, accuses them of failing to share their food with each other (1 Corinthians 11.17). And if that wasn't enough then there were periods of persecution and Roman laws against the meetings of religious societies which made a full-scale meal difficult to organize. So it's not surprising that in our earliest full account of a Eucharist outside the New Testament,

given by Justin Martyr at Rome in the middle of the second century, arrangements are very different. The eucharistic action (taking, blessing, breaking and giving) has now become separated from a meal. It is an early morning service instead of a Sunday evening assembly, and prayers, readings and a sermon have been added to it, based on what happened in the synagogue and forming what we now know as the Liturgy of the Word. Justin referred to both the service and the elements of bread and wine as 'eucharist'.

There had always been the tendency to link the Eucharist with the sacrificial death of Christ. There are several reasons for this.

❖ The Last Supper had taken place near or at the time of the Passover when the lambs were slain as a sacrifice;

❖ The meal occurred so near to the time of Jesus' own death;

❖ Jesus spoke of the bread as his Body which was given and of the wine as his Blood which was shed so that sins could be forgiven, just as some of the Jewish sacrifices were for the forgiveness of sins.

So when Christians broke bread and drank wine in remembrance of Jesus, they remembered his sacrifice on the cross. During the second century, some leading Christians began to see the Eucharist as not only remembering the death of Jesus but actually making present here and now his offering of himself to the Father. Christ was seen as both the priest and the victim at the sacrifice that was being offered, and the bread and wine were strongly identified with his Body and Blood.

DISCUSSION

Read the following passages from Luke's Gospel: Luke 9.10–17, Luke 21.14–19, Luke 24.13–35

❖ Do you detect any common features that might contribute to the way Christians understand the Holy Communion service?

❖ Have you ever experienced Holy Communion in the context of a meal (sometimes called an 'agape')? What were the advantages and disadvantages of worshipping in this way?

After the conversion of Constantine in the fourth century, Christianity became the state religion and acquired many of the rich trappings of the former pagan worship. The Holy Communion became an elaborate ceremony with processions, vestments and a complex series of chants – a great spectacle worthy of the state religion of the Roman Empire. The thinking about the service developed as well. Because of the Arian and other heresies of the fourth century which tended to deny that Christ was fully divine, great emphasis was placed on the divinity of Christ in the sacrament. This led to a growing reverence for the Holy

Communion which encouraged people to prepare themselves spiritually before receiving the bread and the wine. In time, this sense of reverence came to be overstressed, so that many people felt themselves unworthy to be communicants, and gave up receiving Communion altogether.

 DISCUSSION
Do you think that in your church people are over-reverent or over-casual about receiving Communion?

THE MIDDLE AGES

[SEE VISUAL 2]

The Middle Ages saw two main changes in how the Eucharist was celebrated. The first was the growth in private Masses. In the sixth century, monks began to be sent as missionaries into northern Europe, and if they were to bring the sacraments with them then they had to be ordained. This led to the foundation of a large number of new monasteries in these parts, filled with great numbers of priests who could not all gather around the altar together, and so those who wished to say Mass daily began to do so privately. In addition, Masses (known as 'votive' Masses) were offered for particular people or concerns, in exchange for which the priest received some sort of payment. As a result of these practices the essential community element of the Eucharist began to be lost.

The second change was strictly speaking just the opposite – a failure to change at all. The service remained in Latin – even when it was celebrated in countries where few people could understand it. Thus it became a religious performance to watch and listen to, rather than a liturgy in which to participate. Through the ceremony people understood that the bread and wine became the Body and Blood of Christ, to be worshipped from afar but not approached. No longer was the Communion a meal, heavenly food, but rather an object of devotion. And through the action of the priest, Christ's sacrifice of himself was seen as being offered to the Father, so that those for whom it was offered might gain the benefits of his Passion, whether they were present or absent, alive or dead.

During the same period there was also a development in how people understood the words of institution ('This is my Body/Blood'). Writers and preachers were anxious to know in precisely what sense the bread and wine 'were' the Body and Blood of Christ. Some theologians took the words in a spiritual sense: Christ was spiritually present in the bread and wine, and the sacrament was a sign of the spiritual world. But the bread and the wine remained bread and wine. On the other extreme some believed that after the consecration the real flesh and blood of Christ were physically present on the altar: the same flesh and blood that Christ had assumed when he became a human being. Stories developed of how the host (the consecrated bread) had even been seen to bleed.

The greatest of the medieval theologians and philosophers, Thomas Aquinas, suggested another way to understand the words 'This is my Body'. His doctrine called **transubstantiation** has been a very influential one, and remains the official teaching of the Roman Catholic Church. Aquinas took what he knew of the Greek philosopher Aristotle and applied it to Christian theology.

Aristotle believed that every object and living thing in the world was made up of two parts – what it was in its essence, which he called the *substance* of a thing, and what it looked like, sounded like, tasted like, and all its outward appearances, which he called the *accidents* of a thing. So the accidents of a chair include its colour, whether it has a back or not, and so on. These accidents could change, but they would not affect the 'chairness' of the object. So too with bread, its accidents include its taste and look, and the way it melts in the mouth if it's unleavened, and so on. Its substance is its breadness. Now, argued Aquinas, before the consecration the bread tastes like bread, looks like bread, and is bread. After the consecration it tastes like bread, looks like bread, and is the Body of Christ. The substance has changed, it has been 'transubstantiated' into another dimension of reality. This is not just a spiritual change, nor is it a physical change that could be perceived by the senses, but it is a metaphysical change that could be perceived by a mind enlightened by faith. As Aquinas put it in the words (translated) of his own hymn:

> Word made Flesh, by word he maketh
> Very bread his Flesh to be;
> Man in wine Christ's Blood partaketh:
> And if senses fail to see,
> Faith alone the true heart waketh
> To behold the mystery.

 DISCUSSION
Is Aquinas' doctrine of transubstantiation a helpful one for the Church today? How would you begin to try to explain what happens (if anything) to the bread and wine during the Eucharistic Prayer?

THE REFORMATION AND BEYOND

[SEE VISUAL 3]

The sixteenth-century Reformation in the West (Luther, Calvin and their contemporaries) tried to restore the Holy Communion to what was thought to be its New Testament form and purpose – the eating of bread and drinking of wine to remember Christ's death with thanksgiving. The reformers rejected the idea that Christ was in any sense offered as a sacrifice in the service, and most, except for Lutherans and some Anglicans, rejected the idea that any transformation took place in the bread and wine themselves, and generally thought instead that Christ was present only to the worthy communicant through the reception of the elements. So the emphasis moved from the consecration of the elements to receiving them in Communion. 'Do this in remembrance of me' – when the medieval churchmen said these words what they were doing in remembrance of Christ was elevating the host, and offering the sacrifice of Christ to the Father. When the reformers said them, what they were referring to was eating bread and drinking wine feeding on Christ in their hearts by faith with thanksgiving.

This is where the *Book of Common Prayer* of 1662, or rather, its predecessors of 1549 and 1552, fit into the picture. Thomas Cranmer, who was the inspiration behind both of the sixteenth-century books, was greatly influenced by the reformers of the Continent, and shared with them the stress on receiving Communion as the climax of the Eucharist, or Lord's Supper as he preferred to call it. His aim was to link the words of Christ – 'Do this in remembrance of me' – as closely as possible with receiving the sacrament, and that's why in our *Book of Common Prayer* (reproduced as Holy Communion Order Two in *Common Worship*), the distribution of Holy Communion comes immediately after the account of the words of Jesus at the Last Supper. To accomplish this Cranmer had to alter the received shape of both the Eucharist in general and the Eucharistic Prayer in particular and it is only during the latter part of the twentieth century that Anglican services have recaptured that traditional shape. (See Session 8 of this course and Holy Communion Order One of *Common Worship*).

Since the time of Cranmer there have been those within the Church of England and the wider Anglican Communion who follow the teaching of the Protestant reformers as far as the Holy Communion is concerned, who stress the reception of Communion, deny that any transformation takes place in the bread and the wine, are suspicious of ceremonial of any kind, and are unhappy with any talk of sacrifice, except the one made once for all by Christ on Calvary. Others have sought to preserve elements of the medieval Catholic tradition, including the adoration of the Blessed Sacrament and the sacrificial aspect of the Mass. Even today Anglicans have many different opinions about what the Holy Communion is all about, or at least, which of its many meanings are the most important. A guiding principle in the recent process of liturgical revision has been to produce words for worship that are usable by all Anglicans, especially in dealing with such subjects as the presence of Christ in the Holy Communion service.

THE EUCHARISTIC PRAYER

[SEE HANDOUT]

At the heart of the service is the prayer of thanksgiving and praise led by the president, in which we recall how Jesus himself gave thanks for the bread and wine and commanded that this action should be continued by his disciples in remembrance of him. From the earliest centuries of the Christian era this **Eucharistic Prayer** has generally contained a number of sections which can be clearly identified. (The detailed discussion below is based on Prayer A of *Common Worship: Holy Communion Order One* but the *Common Worship* prayers do not share an identical shape and structure.)

The introductory dialogue

The prayer begins with a short dialogue between the president and the people. Like the Jewish forms of thanksgiving from which it is derived the participants are asked to remember God, and to give thanks for his mercies. In all its Christian forms the basic content remains the same: mutual greeting; an invitation to lift up the heart to God, with a response that the people are doing so;

an invitation to give thanks, with a response that declares the rightness and duty of doing so.

> The Lord be with you
> **and also with you.**

The president and people greet each other and recognize their roles, as they have at the beginning of the Holy Communion service. (See Session 8.) Together they are about to give thanks to God, and this greeting sets up the relationship between them. The alternative

> The Lord is here.
> **His Spirit is with us.**

recognizes the role of God's Spirit in the hearts of the worshippers as they move towards the climax of the service.

> Lift up your hearts.
> **We lift them to the Lord.**

The president invites the congregation to lift their hearts and minds into the heavenly places, the true place of Christian worship, as the New Testament reminds us so often (for example, throughout the Book of Revelation). This theme will be taken up again when we reach the Sanctus.

> Let us give thanks to the Lord our God.
> **It is right to give thanks and praise.**

This is the principal purpose of the Eucharistic Prayer – to give thanks – just as thanksgiving should be one of the keynotes of Christian life in general. And so the next part of the prayer begins to do just that.

The Preface

This term refers to the material in this particular prayer up to but not including the Sanctus ('Holy, holy, holy, Lord'), although in some of the other prayers it continues after the Sanctus. The word 'preface' is a rather misleading word. When used in secular contexts it means something that comes before the main text of a book. But it is here a translation of the Latin *praefatio* which means 'proclamation'. Right at the start of the great prayer the Christian community proclaims what God has done, and why it is that they want to give him thanks and praise.

All Christian praise is offered through Jesus Christ, because it is through him that God has done all that he has done. In particular, thanks is given for three things:

1. for creating the world and giving life to his people – the work of God in creation;

2. for giving his Son to die and to be raised from the dead, so freeing humankind from the slavery of sin – the love of God in redemption;

3. for sending the Holy Spirit and creating a people for his praise – the power of God in the calling into being of the Church.

The prayers of Order One vary in how much is said about each of these aspects which together make up the whole sweep of what is known as salvation history. Some of the prayers contain a much fuller narrative than the three short paragraphs of this prayer.

But sometimes there will be a particular thing for which we want to give God thanks – depending on what time of the year it is, or what the theme of the service has been. So *Common Worship* provides a selection of special material, known as 'Proper' Prefaces ('proper' in the sense of appropriate), which can be used either instead of the whole of the usual preface (the 'extended prefaces' suitable for Prayers A, B and E), or in addition to it (the 'shorter prefaces').

The Sanctus and Benedictus

Thanksgiving spills over into adoration. Having praised God for all his acts the worshippers are allowed for a brief moment to praise him for himself, to join their voices for a moment with the worship of heaven. The **Sanctus** – 'Holy, holy, holy' – is based on Isaiah's vision in the temple, and has been a feature of Eucharistic Prayers since the fourth century.

The **Benedictus** ('Blessed is he . . .') has had a long association with the Sanctus, but was dropped by Cranmer in 1552, because the language of the triumphal entry into Jerusalem may have suggested a very physical coming of Christ in the Eucharist. Its use is now optional.

The Post-Sanctus 'link' including a preliminary *epiclesis*

First of all, what is an *epiclesis*? It is the moment when the president asks for the coming of God's transforming Holy Spirit. In the Eastern Orthodox Churches this section comes almost at the end of the prayer (as is true of its position also within *Common Worship* Prayers D, F, G and H), while in the West it has generally appeared at this point (as in *Common Worship* Prayers A, B, C and E). In the rites of Orthodox and Roman Catholic Christians the *epiclesis* asks specifically that the gifts of bread and wine will be transformed into the Body and Blood of Christ. Many Anglicans are happier to link the work of the Spirit with the people who will receive the elements rather than so closely with the elements themselves.

'and as we follow his example and obey his command,
grant that by the power of your Holy Spirit
these gifts of bread and wine
may be to us his body and his blood;'

(Order One, Prayer A)

The Institution narrative

The text, which varies from prayer to prayer, is based on the account in 1 Corinthians and is central to the narrative of the whole Eucharistic Prayer. It attaches the actual celebration that is happening now to the Lord's original command: it says that *this* remembrance feast is *that* which he instituted the night that he was betrayed.

The *Anamnesis*

This is an almost untranslatable word. Memorial, commemoration, remembrance – all these suggest that the person commemorated is past and absent, whereas *anamnesis* means exactly the opposite; the person or event commemorated is actually made present, is brought into the realm of the here and now. So Christians remember in this special way Christ's death, resurrection and ascension, and look forward to his second coming, linking past, present and future together in the timeless moment of the Communion service. And as they remember, they also do something. They do not immediately, as in *The Book of Common Prayer*, receive the consecrated elements. Nor do they, as in the Roman Catholic rite, offer the Body and Blood of Christ to the Father as a sacrifice. They do something which is carefully phrased, so as not to commit the Church of England to one particular view:

'we make the memorial of Christ your Son our Lord'.

(Order One, Prayer A)

In several of the prayers the congregation then link themselves with this moment of *anamnesis* as they join in one of the memorial acclamations for Christ's person and his work and expected return. [SEE VISUAL 4]

DISCUSSION

Which of the memorial acclamations do you prefer, and why?

Prayer for fruitful reception

'Accept through him, our great high priest,
this our sacrifice of thanks and praise . . .'

As the congregation celebrates Christ's sacrifice made once for all upon the cross, they also make an offering, a sacrifice, one of thanks and praise, a spiritual sacrifice. Notice that they pray for it to be accepted through Christ, but there is no suggestion that they are offering Christ to the Father, only asking that their weak and imperfect offering will be seen through the merciful eyes of the one who made the perfect offering.

Then the prayer moves towards the moment of receiving Holy Communion, and prays for some of the benefits which the worshippers hope to receive by it.

'and as we eat and drink these holy gifts
in the presence of your divine majesty,
renew us by your Spirit,
inspire us with your love,
and unite us in the body of your Son,
Jesus Christ our Lord.'

Just as the worshippers have asked the Spirit to be with them at an earlier point as they recalled Christ's death, now they ask to be renewed by the same Spirit as they share in Communion, and they pray for unity, a unity reflected in God himself, as the final section of the prayer makes clear.

Doxology

This sense of unity in time and space, that the worshippers have also experienced at the Sanctus, is taken up again in a great upward sweep of praise, as they are caught up together in the worship of heaven.

session 9 – HANDOUT

Eucharistic Prayer A

The Lord be with you   (or)   The Lord is here.
and also with you.   **His Spirit is with us.**

Lift up your hearts.
We lift them to the Lord.

Let us give thanks to the Lord our God.
It is right to give thanks and praise.

PREFACE

It is indeed right,
it is our duty and our joy,
at all times and in all places
to give you thanks and praise,
holy Father, heavenly King,
almighty and eternal God,
through Jesus Christ your Son our Lord.

*The following may be omitted
if a short proper preface is used*

For he is your living Word;
through him you have created all things
    from the beginning,
and formed us in your own image.

[To you be glory and praise for ever.]

> Praise for creation

Through him you have freed us
    from the slavery of sin,
giving him to be born of a woman
and to die upon the cross;
you raised him from the dead
and exalted him to your right hand
    on high.

[To you be glory and praise for ever.]

> Praise for redemption

Through him you have sent upon us
your holy and life-giving Spirit,
and made us a people
    for your own possession.

[To you be glory and praise for ever.]

> Praise for sanctification

Short proper preface, when appropriate

Therefore with angels and archangels,
and with all the company of heaven,
we proclaim your great and glorious name,
for ever praising you and saying:

> Proper Preface

**Holy, holy, holy Lord,
God of power and might,
heaven and earth are full of your glory.
Hosanna in the highest.
[Blessed is he who comes in the
    name of the Lord.
Hosanna in the highest.]**

> SANCTUS and BENEDICTUS

Accept our praises, heavenly Father,
through your Son our Saviour Jesus Christ,

and as we follow his example
    and obey his command,
grant that by the power of your Holy Spirit
these gifts of bread and wine
may be to us his body and his blood;

> Link, including preliminary 'EPICLESIS'

who in the same night that
    he was betrayed,
took bread and gave you thanks;
he broke it and gave it
    to his disciples, saying:
Take, eat; this is my body
    which is given for you;
do this in remembrance of me.

[To you be glory and praise for ever.]

> NARRATIVE OF INSTITUTION

In the same way, after supper
he took the cup and gave you thanks;
he gave it to them, saying:
Drink this, all of you;
this is my blood of the new covenant,
which is shed for you and for many
for the forgiveness of sins.
Do this, as often as you drink it,
in remembrance of me.

[To you be glory and praise for ever.]

Therefore, heavenly Father,
we remember his offering of himself
made once for all upon the cross;
we proclaim his mighty resurrection
and glorious ascension;
we look for the coming of your kingdom,
and with this bread and this cup
we make the memorial of Christ
    your Son our Lord.

Great is the mystery of Faith
Christ has died... etc.

> 'ANAMNESIS'

Accept through him, our great high priest,
this our sacrifice of thanks and praise,
and as we eat and drink these holy gifts
in the presence of your divine majesty,
renew us by your Spirit,
inspire us with your love
and unite us in the body of your Son,
Jesus Christ our Lord.

[To you be glory and praise for ever.]

> Prayer for fruitful reception and secondary 'EPICLESIS'

Through him, and with him, and in him
in the unity of the Holy Spirit,
with all who stand before you
    in earth and heaven,
we worship you, Father almighty,
in songs of everlasting praise:

**Blessing and honour and glory and power be
yours for ever and ever. Amen.**

> 'DOXOLOGY'

Before the next session

In Jesus Christ, God is 'overthrowing an order of life corrupted by sin and death and bringing to birth a renewed creation, a creation alive with the healing presence of God's Spirit'. (*Common Worship: Wholeness and Healing*: Theological Introduction)

In preparation for this session look up the following Bible references and see how they illustrate this perception of salvation:

Luke 4:18–21	Romans 3:21–26	Luke 12:50
Colossians 1:15-27	John 9 (especially v. 3)	Romans 8:34, 18–30

1

DIFFERENT NAMES FOR COMMUNION

The Lord's Supper

Holy Communion

THE EUCHARIST

The Liturgy

The Mass

THE HOLY MYSTERIES

2

FROM SUPPER TO SACRAMENT

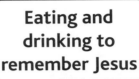

Eating and drinking to remember Jesus

Evening (1 Cor. 11)

– – – – – – – – AD 100

Shared meals

Evening

Word
....
'Eucharist'

Morning

3

PRAYER BOOK 'EUCHARISTIC' STRUCTURE

DIALOGUE	• 'Lift up your hearts'
PRAISE	• 'It is very meet…'
SANCTUS	• 'Holy, holy, holy…'
HUMBLE ACCESS	• 'We do not presume…'
PRAYER	• '…grant that we… may be partakers…'
INSTITUTION	• 'Do this in remembrance of me…'
RECEPTION	• Remembering by doing
PRAYER	• Thanks or self-offering
DOXOLOGY	• Gloria in Excelsis

4

FOUR MEMORIAL 'ACCLAMATIONS'

[Great is the mystery of faith:]
Christ has died:
Christ is risen:
Christ will come again.

[Praise to you, Lord Jesus:]
Dying you destroyed our death,
rising you restored our life:
Lord Jesus, come in glory

[Christ is the bread of life:]
When we eat this bread
and drink this cup,
we proclaim your death,
Lord Jesus,
until you come in glory.

[Jesus Christ is Lord:]
Lord, by your cross and resurrection
you have set us free.
You are the Saviour of the world.

WHOLENESS AND HEALING

PART A – GETTING STARTED

Aim

To explore the place of services and prayer for wholeness, healing and reconciliation in Church of England worship and to consider the *Common Worship* texts.

Leader's preparation

Read the Theological Introduction to the Services of Wholeness and Healing in *Common Worship: Pastoral Services*, p.9. It would be helpful to look up all the Bible references (cf. the group's 'before the next session' task). You may like to make copies of the whole Introduction available for group reference. Make yourself familiar with the *Common Worship* provisions for wholeness and healing, as this session explores them in some detail. You will also need to look through the service for the 'Visitation of the Sick' in *The Book of Common Prayer*.

Opening worship

Read aloud Colossians 1.15–23a.

Sing, listen to or read aloud a hymn or song about healing and forgiveness, such as 'Dear Lord and Father of Mankind' (J. G. Whittier) or 'Be still', for the presence of the Lord' (David Evans).

Session starter

What did the Bible references studied by the group members before the session have to say about 'wholeness and healing'?

What images or ideas particularly struck group members? Why?

PART B – HEART OF THE MATTER

See pages 84–7

PART C – TAKING IT FURTHER

For further discussion

The *Common Worship* services and prayers for 'Wholeness and Healing' are printed in *Common Worship: Pastoral Services* and not in the main book. This might restrict awareness of these services to the clergy and other ministers. How might lay members of the Church be encouraged to discover this important and helpful new spiritual provision?

One of the *Common Worship* services is called 'A Celebration of Wholeness and Healing'. That might be seen to indicate an understanding of wholeness that could make some people feel 'less than whole' – spiritually, as well as physically and mentally. How can we celebrate these services so that this doesn't happen?

Reading and resources

Common Worship: Pastoral Services (Church House Publishing, 2000). Includes the complete texts for the services of Wholeness and Healing.

Davies, John, *Affirming Confession* (DLT, 1998). A sensitive exploration of sacramental confession as a helpful part of the Church's ministry of pastoral and spiritual care today.

Dudley, Martin, *Humanity and Healing: Ministering to the Sick in the Catholic Tradition,* (DLT, 1998). This short book gives helpful background information for those who would like to know more about the history, theology and practice of services for wholeness and healing.

Dudley, Martin and Rowell, Geoffrey (eds) *Confession and Absolution* (SPCK, 1990).

Dudley, Martin and Rowell, Geoffrey (eds) *The Oil of Gladness* (SPCK, 1993). Each of these books provides a thorough and authoritative study of their subject from an Anglican perspective.

Headley, C. *The Laying on of Hands in the Parish Healing Ministry* (Grove, 1988, Worship Series no. 104). A practical introduction to the ministry of the laying on of hands, in the context of biblical, historical and pastoral perspectives.

Perham, Michael (ed.) *Liturgy for a New Century* (ch. 7) (SPCK, 1991). Short occasional essays which explored new possibilities for Church of England liturgy while the *Common Worship* services were still in preparation. Interesting to compare the ideas of 1991 with the realities of *Common Worship*.

Closing worship

Use the two sections 'Prayer and Penitence' and 'The Sending Out' from 'A Celebration of Wholeness and Healing' (*Pastoral Services* pages 17 and 23). (In the absence of a priest, use an alternative prayer to the prayer of absolution, such as the Collect for Trinity 21.)

Before the next session – Marriage

What was the 'best' and what was the 'worst' church marriage service you have attended (liturgically speaking)? What was so good and what was so bad about each one?

May you believe and trust that the only name under heaven given for health and salvation is the name of our Lord Jesus Christ.

PART B – HEART OF THE MATTER

SOMETHING NEW?

The *Common Worship* book of Pastoral Services contains a large section of services and prayers for 'Wholeness and Healing'. For those of us brought up on the simple diet of a normal Sunday run of Church of England services from the *Book of Common Prayer* and the *Alternative Service Book (1980)*, this whole section of *Common Worship* may initially strike us as something new and strange. Services and prayers for wholeness and healing have, however, always been part of Church of England worship. There are, for example, several such services tucked away in the lesser-read corners of our Prayer Books or, in the case of the *Alternative Service Book (1980)*, appended in a separate booklet.

Hidden, for example, in the *Book of Common Prayer*, between the 'Form of Solemnization of Matrimony' and the 'Order for the Burial of the Dead' are two now infrequently used orders of service, for the 'Visitation of the Sick' and for the 'Communion of the Sick'. And, linked with the *Alternative Service Book (1980)*, there is a commended collection of 'alternative' services and prayers for use for 'Ministry to the Sick'.

DISCUSSION
Have any members of the group experienced services of ministry to the sick, either for themselves or with others?
Why is the Church's ministry to the sick so important?

Throughout the twentieth century gentle pressure built up in the Church of England for a more developed ministry of healing in parish worship. This was regularly discussed at Lambeth Conferences from 1908, and in 1935 official rites of healing were commended for use in the Church of England. These services incorporated the laying on of hands and anointing. At first, the celebration of such services happened in relatively few churches. Since those early days, however, services of wholeness and healing have been further developed and more widely used. The *Common Worship* services of Wholeness and Healing balance this Anglican tradition with contemporary charismatic and Catholic insights and practice.

EXPLORING *COMMON WORSHIP*: SERVICES OF WHOLENESS AND HEALING

'Healing, reconciliation and restoration are integral to the good news of Jesus Christ. For this reason, prayer for individuals, focused through laying on of hands or anointing with oil, has a proper place within the public prayer of the Church. God's gracious activity of healing is to be seen both as part of the proclaiming of the good news and as an outworking of the presence of the Spirit in the life of the Church.' (*Theological Introduction: Wholeness and Healing*)

[VISUAL 1 – WHOLENESS AND HEALING]

There are three forms of service and two sets of prayers as well as some supplementary texts, Bible readings and prayers. Each service includes prayer for healing and emphasizes the Church's wider celebration of reconciliation and renewal in the Gospel of Christ. The provisions include:

1. a diocesan or deanery celebration of wholeness and healing;

2. laying on of hands with prayer and anointing – a resource for occasional use in the context of Holy Communion services in the parish;

3. guidelines for prayer for individuals in public worship – not for healing services specifically, but for churches where prayer for individuals is offered as part of, or after, Sunday worship;

4. ministry to the sick – a set of services intended for use in the sick-room, hospital or hospice, which includes Holy Communion with the sick and housebound;

5. some prayers for protection and peace for use by or with individuals at need.

DEANERY AND DIOCESAN CELEBRATIONS OF WHOLENESS AND HEALING

Most of us have lived happily without such deanery and diocesan services throughout our Christian lives and might well want to ask whether there really is a place or a need for such celebrations! Yet this form of service is placed first in the *Common Worship* services of Wholeness and Healing. Why?

The service celebrates wholeness and healing in the wider context of diocesan and deanery worship. Its regular, not necessarily frequent, use within diocese and deanery should help to keep the Gospel proclamation of wholeness, renewal and reconciliation at the forefront of worshippers' spiritual consciousness.

❖ **Collect** The special Collect sets the tone of the service:

> Heavenly Father, you anointed your Son Jesus Christ with the Holy Spirit and with power to bring us the blessings of your kingdom. Anoint your Church with the same Holy Spirit, that we who share in his suffering and victory may bear witness to the gospel of salvation.

❖ **Intercession and Penitence** The Prayers of Intercession express our human need for wholeness and healing. The Prayers of Penitence acknowledge our responsibility for the destructive nature of our sin and pray for restoration. The ministry of reconciliation is highlighted and emphasizes that wholeness requires God to restore us from our sinful state.

[SEE HANDOUT]

❖ **Laying on of Hands and Anointing** There is a powerful prayer over the oil to be used in anointing. The prayer speaks of the renewal brought by God the Holy Spirit, of Jesus the Anointed One, of the biblical ministry of anointing, and of the needs of those who are sick today. Members of the congregation are invited to receive the laying on of hands with prayer and anointing, for themselves or on behalf of others.

❖ **The Sending Out** The service ends with celebration and joy. The Lord's Prayer is said, a short Gospel passage is proclaimed, the Peace – the sign of the restoration of community – is shared, and the congregation is dismissed.

> Go in the joy and peace of Christ.
> **Thanks be to God.**

DISCUSSION

Why is it so important for Christian worship to celebrate God's gifts of wholeness, healing and reconciliation?

In what ways do you think regular services of wholeness and healing in your deanery or diocese could encourage and support your congregation and the worship in your church?

WHOLENESS AND HEALING: PARISH SERVICES

[VISUAL 2 – A PARISH HEALING SERVICE]

The central parish service of wholeness and healing is the 'Laying on of Hands with Prayer and Anointing at a Celebration of the Holy Communion'. It is intended for occasional, not weekly use, though it could become part of a parish's regular programme of Sunday services.

It is a clearly structured Holy Communion Service including the laying on of hands with prayer and anointing. These would normally follow immediately after the intercessions. The order and structure is the familiar order and structure of the *Common Worship* Holy Communion Service. (See Session 8.) The seasonal feel can be maintained if it is felt to be appropriate, or the theme of healing may be extended into the wider service.

❖ **Litany of Healing** The first indication of the theme of healing comes with the litany of healing. (See handout.)

This prayer addresses the need of all Christians for healing and forgiveness; sin is seen as one cause of some of the situations needing healing and wholeness.

❖ **Laying on of Hands with Prayer and Anointing** If there is to be anointing as well as the laying on of hands, a prayer is said over the oil. God is blessed in this prayer, and the people who will receive anointing are prayed for. (The oil for anointing may be from oil previously blessed by the bishop at a special service.) Those receiving the ministry of the laying on of hands with prayer and anointing would come forward immediately after this prayer, or during the Communion. The words used stress 'Christ's healing touch' and 'Christ's forgiveness, healing and love'.

The rubrics advise that only a priest may anoint, but the president may to ask other people to assist with the laying on of hands and prayer. After this, a prayer said by the president moves the service on towards the Peace and the Liturgy of the Sacrament.

> 'May you believe and trust that the only Name under heaven given for health and salvation, is the Name of our Lord Jesus Christ.'

The Holy Communion service then proceeds as usual.

Elements of the service will be new to many, but most members of the Church of England should feel able to engage with the words, actions and the structure of the service. The Eucharist is unchanged; the ministry of wholeness and healing will normally be exercised at the familiar communion rail; the president will be the local minister, possibly with one or two trusted parish lay ministers assisting.

How might this service go down in the parish, especially if there has been no previous experience of doing something like this? The only way for that to be discovered is by doing it! But the combination of the familiar context of Holy Communion with the special attention given in the service to the needs for forgiveness and healing that are common to all worshippers should ensure that most parishes will find these services encouraging and enriching.

DISCUSSION

Is the ministry of the laying on of hands with prayer and anointing at Holy Communion a possibility in your parish?

How would you feel about it?

In what way might it be introduced into your Parish Communion services so that it is welcomed, not feared, by the congregation?

If used on a regular basis, what do you think the long-term effects might be? (Use Visual 3, Images of Wholeness and Healing to assists your discussion.)

or

If you already incorporate services of wholeness and healing in the worship life of your parish, how might you use *Common Worship* material to enrich and enhance your services?

Do you feel that your church's experience of regularly celebrating services of wholeness and healing has had a wider impact on the life of your church and on individual Christian formation in the long term?

MINISTRY WITH THE SICK AND HOUSEBOUND

Ministry with those who are sick, housebound or in residential care is very important in parish life. There are provisions in the *Common Worship* services that will help the Church with this aspect of parish ministry.

The provision for 'Ministry to the Sick' is focused on the celebration of the Holy Communion, (or the distribution of consecrated bread and wine). The services are relatively short. The basic structure is that of the *Common Worship* Communion service, with special additional prayers for the laying on of hands and anointing.

These services for the sick and housebound assume a shared ministry between clergy and lay ministers and should encourage ministers to invite more church members to share this ministry with them. Lay persons so authorized by the bishop may distribute consecrated bread and wine to the sick and housebound, and, if pastorally appropriate, in residential homes.

'The Church of God, of which we are members, has taken bread and wine and given thanks over them according to our Lord's command. These holy gifts are now offered to us, that with faith and thanksgiving, we may share in the communion of the body and blood of Christ.' (*These words are said by authorized lay ministers when distributing consecrated bread and wine to the sick and housebound.*)

DISCUSSION

The *Book of Common Prayer* 'Visitation of the Sick' service suggests that the purpose of the minister's visit is to help the sick person respond to 'God's visitation' of him in his sickness. The minister would pray with and for him in his sickness, and, before commending him to God, examine him as to his spiritual health, encouraging him to take the necessary actions to restore his spiritual health: confess his sins, make his will, settle his temporal estates and, as he was able, be liberal to the poor.

Should clergy visiting the sick today be motivated by the same purposes? What other purpose might there be?

PRAYERS FOR PROTECTION AND PEACE

There is a small collection of prayers for protection and peace that ministers may use to pray with those suffering from a sense of disturbance and unrest (*Pastoral Services* p. 95). The prayers are carefully crafted; some are biblical, others come as tried and tested prayers from within the Christian tradition.

There are prayers 'for a person or persons', 'for a place', 'before sleep', and 'as a blessing'. The Celtic tradition of prayer, helpful to many today, was evidently a strong influence in some of the prayers.

May the cross of the Son of God,
which is mightier than all the hosts of Satan,
and more glorious than all the hosts of heaven,
abide with me in my going out and my coming in.
By day and by night, at morning and at evening,
at all times and in all places may it protect and defend me . . .

Pastoral Services p. 94

While the prayers do respond to peoples' experiences of fear, of vulnerability, of enslaving passions, of wickedness and the sense of evil, they are not prayers of exorcism and deliverance. (The accompanying notes stress that the ministry of deliverance may only be exercised by priests authorized by the bishop and under his direction.)

DISCUSSION

Think about the times when you have needed, for yourself or others, prayers of protection and peace. You might share something of these memories within the group.

How might the prayers of protection and peace in *Common Worship* be used in order to help others facing similar experiences?

RECONCILIATION

[VISUAL 4 – RECONCILIATION]

One of the intentions of the Liturgical Commission in *Common Worship*, both in the Services of Wholeness and Healing and in the Initiation Services, was to help people see the connection between spiritual and physical wholeness. Sin damages spiritual health, so forgiveness and reconciliation are important aspects of restoration to spiritual wholeness.

Whenever Christians come to God in worship, prayers of penitence and reconciliation are therefore essential. In the presence of God, people are all too aware of their imperfections and sin, much of which is their own deliberate fault. They know that they are less 'holy', less whole, than they ought to be.

When Christians confess their sins they acknowledge their personal responsibility for the damage and hurt they have caused, and they are saying sorry – to God, to the Church and to the community. They seek God's forgiveness, his guidance and his blessing. And all this with the desire that God will put wrong things right and that lives may be lived in the future in the way that God wants.

One way of understanding penitential prayer is that it is prayer for restoration to full spiritual health and wholeness. In that spiritual 'ill health' damages others and damages creation, so the restoration of spiritual health restores spiritual health and wholeness to others. The ministry of reconciliation is therefore a public as well as a private matter.

The way the Church exercises the ministry of reconciliation is very important. While 'general' confession is part of every act of worship and serves most people's spiritual needs, there are occasions when people need more specific help to see, acknowledge and turn from what they have done wrong. This may be particularly important at major crisis points in life. The Prayer Book, for example, in its prayers for the 'Visitation of the Sick' makes provision for 'special' confession. This is a more detailed acknowledgement of our serious sins, made to God, but in the presence of a priest.

Here shall the sick person be moved to make a special confession of his sins, if he feel his conscience troubled with any weighty matter. After which confession, the Priest shall absolve him (if he humbly and heartily desire it) after this sort.

Our Lord Jesus Christ, who hath left power to his Church to absolve all sinners who truly repent and believe in him, of his great mercy forgive thee thine offences: and by his authority committed to me, I absolve thee from all thy sins, In the Name of the Father, and of the Son, and of the Holy Ghost. Amen.

(The Order for the Visitation of the Sick, *Book of Common Prayer* 1662)

Lent and Advent are traditionally times in the Church's year when it is particularly appropriate for Christians to be mindful of their tendency to sin and their need for penitence. Two special services of penitence in *Lent, Holy Week, Easter* encourage local congregations to address and respond to these things as a community of Christians, and not just as individuals.

There are no additional special services of reconciliation in any of the new *Common Worship* provisions, though the Liturgical Commission does plan to publish a book of essays and suggested texts for discussion.

DISCUSSION

How do you understand sin? What is 'sin' and what is 'sinful?'

How might the Church better help Christians to acknowledge, confess and receive God's forgiveness of their sins?

BAPTISM AND RESTORATION

Common Worship emphasizes the link between the sacrament of Baptism, the Services of Wholeness and Healing and the Church's ministry of reconciliation.

The first three sentences of the theological introduction to the Services of Wholeness and Healing in *Common Worship* make this clear.

❖ Baptism witnesses to God's gift in salvation . . .

❖ Baptism points to the way in which God in Jesus Christ is overthrowing an old order . . .

❖ Baptism is a sign of individual and corporate forgiveness and renewal.

Wholeness and healing services can therefore be seen as helping Christians move forward in the spiritual journey they began at baptism.

The Church's ministry of wholeness, healing and reconciliation expresses and enables the work of Christ in overthrowing the 'old order of sin and death'. As such it is a ministry of restoration, continually at work to restore in us that newness and wholeness of life that was signified in our baptism.

DISCUSSION

The services and prayers for wholeness and healing might be printed in a new edition of the *Common Worship* Initiation Services, as well as with the Pastoral Services. Can you see why? Do you think this is a good idea?

session 10 – HANDOUT

Closing Worship
PRAYER AND PENITENCE
(from Common Worship *'Celebration of Wholeness and Healing')*

The response: **We praise and bless you, Lord.**

God the Father, your will for all people is health and salvation. **R**

God the Son, you came that we might have life, and might have it more abundantly. **R**

God the Holy Spirit, you make our bodies the temple of your presence. **R**

Holy Trinity, one God, in you we live and move and have our being. **R**

The response: **Hear us, Lord of life.**

Lord, grant your healing grace to all who are sick, injured or disabled, that they may be made whole. **R**

Grant to all who are lonely, anxious or depressed a knowledge of your will and an awareness of your presence. **R**

Grant to all who minister to those who are suffering wisdom and skill, sympathy and patience. **R**

Mend broken relationships, and restore to those in distress soundness of mind and serenity of spirit. **R**

Sustain and support those who seek your guidance, and lift up all who are brought low by the trials of this life. **R**

Grant to the dying peace and a holy death, and uphold by the grace and consolation of your Holy Spirit those who are bereaved. **R**

Restore to wholeness whatever is broken by human sin, in our lives, in our nation, and in the world. **R**

You are the Lord who does mighty wonders.
You have declared your power among the peoples.
With you, Lord, is the well of life.
And in your light do we see light.
Hear us, Lord of life.
Heal us, and make us whole.

A period of silence follows

The gospel calls us to turn away from sin and be faithful to Christ.
As we offer ourselves to him in penitence and faith,
we renew our confidence and trust in his mercy.

There follows a period of silent reflection and self-examination.

Most merciful God,
Father of our Lord Jesus Christ,
we confess that we have sinned
in thought, word and deed.
We have not loved you with our whole heart.
We have not loved our neighbour as ourselves.
In your mercy, forgive what we have been,
help us to amend what we are,
and direct what we shall be;
that we may do justly, love mercy,
and walk humbly with you, our God. Amen.

The leader, if a priest, says an authorized prayer of absolution. A lay leader might use an 'us/we' form of such a prayer, or the Collect for the 21st Sunday after Trinity.

A hymn or song may be sung.

THE PEACE AND DISMISSAL
God has made us one in Christ. He has set his seal upon us, and, as a pledge of what is to come, has given the Spirit to dwell in our hearts.
The peace of the Lord be always with you.

And also with you.

Before the next session
What was the 'best' and what was the 'worst' Church marriage you have attended (liturgically speaking!)? What was so good and what was so bad about each one?

1

WHOLENESS AND HEALING

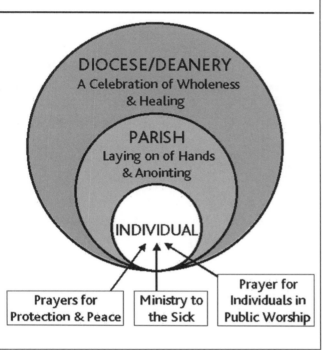

| Prayers for Protection & Peace | Ministry to the Sick | Prayer for Individuals in Public Worship |

2

A PARISH 'HEALING SERVICE'

3

IMAGES OF WHOLENESS AND HEALING

anointing
power
blessings
Spirit
witness
salvation

need
sickness
sin

intercession
penitence
forgiveness
restoration
renewal

joy
peace
thanksgiving

4

RECONCILIATION

I confess that I have sinned, against .....

God
others
Reconciliation
society
creation

Go in peace to love and serve the Lord

MARRIAGE

PART A – GETTING STARTED

Aim

To understand the place of marriage in the worship of the Church, and to explore how its words and symbolism proclaim and support a Christian understanding of marriage in our changing culture.

Leader's preparation

The group will need access to both the *Book of Common Prayer* and *Common Worship* marriage services. Read the two services through before the session and note the differences. Choose appropriate music for the acts of worship. The closing worship suggests prayer for couples preparing for marriage in your church – arrange for the names to be collected.

Opening worship

Listen to or sing the hymn 'Love divine, all loves excelling' (Charles Wesley). Ask someone to read aloud 1 Corinthians 13.1–13. Say together the *Common Worship* Collect for the Second Sunday after Trinity (see handout).

Session starter

What were the good and bad characteristics of marriage ceremonies that people identified in their pre-session thinking? Record on a flip chart or OHP, without too much discussion.

Ask the group what factors make a marriage service 'good'.

Would all couples who get married in church agree with the judgement of the group?

PART B – HEART OF THE MATTER

See pages 92–5

PART C – TAKING IT FURTHER

For further discussion

either

'We need much more than the poor symbols that we have today, with the bride walking to church on her father's arm and returning on her husband's, as if she were a piece of property given away,' (K. Stevenson *The First Rites*). Have the *Common Worship* provisions succeeded in responding to this plea? See Visual 3.

or

In the light of your earlier discussions as to whether the institution of marriage is social or religious, discuss which perspective the *Common Worship* marriage service reflects.

Reading and resources

Authorized and commended marriage (and related) services

The Book of Common Prayer, The Marriage Service (Alternative Services: First Series); *Common Worship: Pastoral Services*.

Books about the Marriage Services

Using Common Worship: Marriage, Stephen Lake (CHP/*Praxis* 2000). A practical guide; helping people make the most of the *Common Worship* services.

Books and Reports about Marriage

Stevenson, Kenneth, *Nuptial Blessing* (Alcuin Club/SPCK, 1982). A thorough study of the history of Christian marriage rites.

Something to Celebrate: Valuing Families in Church and Society (Church House Publishing, 1995). A General Synod (Board of Social Responsibility) report on 'valuing families in Church and society'.

Harvey, Anthony E. *Marriage, Divorce and the Church* (DLT, 1997). A succinct 'pocket book' guide to the history, theology, practice and pastoral considerations relating to marriage and divorce in the Anglican Church. Helps the reader begin to address the difficult questions.

Marriage: A Teaching Document (CHP, 1999). 'Official' Church of England thinking on marriage and remarriage.

Marriage in Church after Divorce (CHP, 2000). A discussion document setting out the issues and a possible way forward.

Closing worship

Read out the names of the couples who are to be married in your church over the coming months – or in the churches of the members of the group. Say together one of the *Common Worship* 'prayers at the calling of the banns'. (*Common Worship: Pastoral Services:* Supplementary Texts, p. 135) (see handout).

Play or sing 'Lead us, heavenly Father, lead us' – or another hymn or song often sung at the end of marriage services.

Before the next session – Funerals

What do you think are the main purposes of the funeral service?

Think about some of the funerals you have attended. What sort of things about them do you remember as being particularly helpful?

What was especially unhelpful or disappointing?

'It is given that as man and woman grow together in love and trust, they shall be united with one another as Christ is united with his Church.'

PART B – HEART OF THE MATTER

'The grace of God in the Holy Spirit is given to all who enter marriage in the conscious desire to hear his call, seeking his strength to live together as they have promised. This is why marriage in the context of worship, properly prepared for by a process of reflection and discussion about the life of faith, is an important ministry of the Church.'

(*Marriage: A Teaching Document*, The House of Bishops, 1999)

CHRISTIAN WORSHIP OR LEGAL CEREMONY?

Is the marriage service 'the joker in the pack' of Church services? (*The First Rites*, K. Stevenson, Lamp 1989.) Wedding services are something of a curious mixture of the secular with the sacred. As in every Christian act of worship, there are Christian words spoken and Christian prayers offered. Christian promises are made in the name of Christ. The service also contains the essential legal ceremonies and forms that the law of the land requires. (See Visual 1.) The officiating minister is, therefore, both the president of a Christian service, and also the registrar of a marriage in law.

In the Church of England this interweaving of legalities and spiritualities is a sort of ritual expression of the identity of a Church 'by law established'. The marriage service of the Established Church has to be available both for the weddings of regular church worshippers as well as for those who, by virtue of living in the parish, have the right to marry in the parish church, even if they are not practising Christians. (This right is only at present available for those who have not been married before, or whose previous marriage has been terminated by death.)

PRIVATE OR PUBLIC?

Marriage is a 'rite of passage' and common to all societies. It is, in its origins at least, a social rather than a religious institution. For this reason it has traditionally been seen as a public event, with the good of the whole community perceived as dependent on it. In the past, contracts between families, dowries, and therefore arranged marriages were major factors.

More recently, however, especially in Western society, marriage has been increasingly understood as a loving relationship between two people, with the contract side of things tending to be private and personal.

In the eyes of the Church, meanwhile, marriage has become more than a social institution; the sense of covenant has become as much if not more important than contract. Thus while the Church of England certainly sees marriage as affirming a mutual belonging and care which strengthens the life of the community as a whole, it increasingly stresses its spiritual and religious nature. This is evident in the contemporary marriage service in the *Alternative Service Book*

(1980) and *Common Worship*; it is also evident in recent statements about marriage and remarriage from the House of Bishops.

The position of the state, however, is interesting. To a large extent marriage in England is generally still seen, and valued, as an important social institution. Yet within English society as a whole there is a rising tide of opinion that such mutual belonging and care is not to be found exclusively within marriage. And it is arguable that it will not be long before such an attitude becomes a 'respectable' position to hold. Is the Church, perhaps, fighting a losing battle in requiring the state to discriminate positively in favour of marriage?

 DISCUSSION
Look at the *Common Worship* Marriage Service and see how it interweaves the spiritual/legal, public/private aspects of marriage. (See Visual 1.) Are the emphases significantly different to those in *The Book of Common Prayer*?

Should the perspective of the Church be influenced by cultural change? What, if anything, is distinctive about Christian marriage?

'A GREAT MYSTERY'

Christians have come to see marriage as displaying something of a sacramental nature. The writer of Ephesians referred to it as 'a great mystery'.

'A man shall leave his father and mother and be joined to his wife, and the two shall become one flesh. This mystery is a profound one, and I am saying that it refers to Christ and the Church.' (Ephesians 5.31, 32)

The pledged relationship of husband and wife has been interpreted to symbolize Christ's love for the Church.

'It is given that as man and woman grow together in love and trust, they shall be united with one another as Christ is united with his Church.' (The Preface to the Marriage Service: *Common Worship*.)

THE HISTORY OF CHRISTIAN MARRIAGE

Before Christ

In pre-Christian days, betrothal was as much a religious ritual as was the marriage itself, both for Jews (cf. Matthew 1.18) and pagans. There are very few descriptions of betrothal and marriage ceremonies in the Bible texts, but we know that the Hebrews saw the relationship between man and woman to be set firmly within God's creative ordering (Genesis 1.27, 28; 2.18–24).

There are several stories in the Hebrew Scriptures that portray Israelite traditions of betrothal and marriage. The story of Isaac and Rebekah, for example, mentions betrothal gifts (Genesis 24.47, 53) and gives the text of a blessing of Rebekah by her own family (Genesis 24.60). The apocryphal Book of Tobit tells an exciting story of the marriage of Tobias and Sarah. There are references to a contract, a marriage feast and texts of prayers.

From other Hebrew sources we know that after a marriage contract was agreed, the betrothal, normally lasting some twelve months, was enacted by a blessing. On the day before the marriage, the couple fasted and prayed, and then appeared wearing crowns of myrtle. The bride, wearing a veil, went to the groom's house for the feast, after which the groom recited the Seven Blessings, a long prayer which gave theological context to the marriage.

Early Christian ceremonies

Early Christian betrothal ceremonies adapted Roman patterns. These included the giving of money in pledge that the ceremony would take place, the gift of a sealing ring to the future wife since she would be in charge of the home, the promise of a dowry, the joining of the couple's hands and the exchanging of a kiss.

The earliest Christian marriages were most probably a development of the Jewish tradition. Roman law permitted the various religions to carry out their own marriage rituals, providing only that both parties consented to the marriage. Christian marriages included a Eucharist and a blessing, and were often followed by an agape, a Christian fellowship meal. The ceremonies took place in people's homes. [VISUAL 2]

DISCUSSION

Our situation today, in relation to secular society, is comparable to that of the early Christians.

Do we have anything to learn from their marriage practices?

Marriage in medieval Europe

Throughout the Middle Ages betrothal was more domestic rite than religious ceremony, though clergy might well be present. There was a simple though formal commitment as the future couple pronounced the words of the promise (*verba de futuro*) – their intention to marry.

As Christianity spread into northern Europe, various local traditions were incorporated into Christian marriages. Rice, for example, was used as a fertility symbol, the bride was given away, bridesmaids were dressed like the bride in order to confuse evil spirits, and a wedding veil was worn as a similar protection. Marriages mostly took place in the home, or even in taverns; the Church's involvement was minimal. The increasing need to have written records of marriages, however, brought about a greater involvement of the Church; priests were among the very few in

the community who were literate and so able to witness and record the ceremony legally. After the wedding, a nuptial Mass was frequently celebrated in the parish church and the parish priest blessed the newly-married couple.

By the twelfth ceremony, wedding ceremonies in England were being held at the church door or porch. It was not until the Reformation that the marriage service took place in the church building. Otherwise, there was little change at the Reformation except that English was used instead of Latin. For a while Puritan objections stopped the use of rings, but this ban did not last for long.

The English Prayer Books

The 1549, 1552 and 1662 marriage services all began with a long address, expanded from the medieval 'banns', which spoke of the institution of Christian marriage, and the reasons for it: in brief, children, continence and company. Cranmer's revised service maintained the traditional division between betrothal and marriage, but conflated it into the one overall ceremony. He introduced the phrase, 'Those whom God hath joined together let no man put asunder'. This, and the declaration of the marriage, were derived from Luther. The exchange of vows took place in the body of the church. After the procession to the altar, prayers were said, a homily was given, and the newly-married persons received the Holy Communion.

Twentieth-century marriage

The 1662 order was the only authorized marriage service in the Church of England right up until the twentieth century. Several modifications, reflecting a changing perception of the marriage relationship, were suggested in the proposed 1928 Prayer Book. Although the 1928 Book was never authorized in its entirety, some of its proposals were authorized in the *Series One* services.

The *Series One* Marriage Service (currently authorized until 2005) differs from *The Book of Common Prayer* Marriage Service in the following respects:

❖ The 'causes for which matrimony was ordained' were reworded (See handout).

❖ An alternative form of the vows was given, where each partner might make the same promise as the other: 'to love and to cherish till death us do part'. The bride no longer had to promise to obey her husband, and the groom, instead of being required to endow his wife with all his worldly goods, was to share them with her;

❖ Holy Communion could follow the marriage ceremony.

DISCUSSION

Look at *The Book of Common Prayer*'s understanding of the 'causes for which matrimony was ordained' (See handout). What order would you put them in today? Would you add any others? Or omit any?

The Alternative Service Book (1980)

Sixty years later, social attitudes with respect to relationships between men and women had changed significantly. The 1980 'alternative' marriage service went some way towards reflecting contemporary culture. The language was modernized; a new preface to the service explained Christian marriage in its contemporary context and reordered the reasons for Christian marriage: mutual comfort, sex within marriage, and children. In this and in other ways the service moved to a greater articulation of the equal status of women and men. Two sets of vows were given; in the first set, the couple made identical promises. No form of words was printed for 'giving away' the bride. The service allowed for more personal touches and offered a choice of Bible readings and prayers.

The 1980 Marriage Service was also 'more religious'. The ministry of the Word and the sermon were given a higher profile.

Common Worship

The *Common Worship* Marriage Service was authorized in 2000. Like the other *Common Worship* Pastoral Services, it does not stand alone but is supported by other services and prayers.

❖ **The Marriage Service** and the Marriage Service within a Celebration of Holy Communion.

❖ **Supplementary Texts** Prayers at the Calling of the Banns; Alternative Preface; Readings and Psalms; Alternative Vows; Prayer at the Giving of the Rings; The Blessing of the Marriage; Additional Prayers and Collects; Canticles.

❖ **Thanksgiving for Marriage.**

THE MARRIAGE SERVICE

The *Common Worship* Marriage Service has quite a different 'feel' to the *Alternative Service Book* service. The language and imagery are richer and more poetic; the service is clearly a celebration of divine and human love. In addition, the actual marriage ceremony is more obviously integrated into the overall act of worship. An outline is also given for the marriage service 'within a celebration of Holy Communion' and some imaginative special texts are given.

The basic Marriage Service falls into two distinct parts: the Introduction and the Marriage. The introductory part of the service prepares couple and congregation for the commitment of marriage. The second part of the service enacts the legal and spiritual ceremonies of the marriage.

The Introduction

The people are welcomed, the service is explained, and declarations from the congregation and the couple are requested. The purpose of the declarations is to ensure that the persons about to marry are legally free to enter into the marriage contract, wish to marry each other and have the support of their families and friends. This latter declaration is a new one: hitherto only the giving away of the bride has indicated an element of 'family consent'. (See handout.) The declarations are normally followed by collect, readings and sermon.

DISCUSSION

Look at the question addressed to the congregation in the first part of the service. (See handout)

Do you see this as a useful addition?

The Marriage

The marriage vows are exchanged and the rings are given. The minister proclaims that the couple are husband and wife and then blesses the marriage. The registration of the marriage may take place at this point or after the prayers.

The notes to the *Common Worship* Marriage Service clarify various options open to the couple and assist with thinking through the implications of making particular choices:

❖ the bride may enter the church escorted by her father or another family member, or the bride and groom may enter church together;

❖ the ceremony of 'giving away' is optional (and the phrase itself is not used) – but alternative suggestions are made in the notes (see handout);

❖ the Prayer Book version of the marriage vows may be used; the bride may make her vow before the bridegroom makes his vow.

DISCUSSION

either

Look at the *Common Worship* Marriage Service from the perspective of two different couples: one couple chooses all the traditional options, the other couple goes for the complete opposite.

Make a list of the significant options chosen, and discuss what the choices seem to reveal about the couples' perception of marriage.

or

What do you think of the various suggestions in the notes to the *Common Worship* service about 'giving away?' (See handout and Visual 3.)

IMAGERY AND SYMBOLISM

All worship is more than mere words, and the *Common Worship* Marriage Service is no exception. Some of the 'blessing of the marriage' prayers, for example, are particularly rich in imagery. Words such as 'let their love for each other be a seal upon their hearts, and a crown upon their heads' make us think of men and women as kings and queens of creation, and remind us of some of the Eastern Orthodox wedding traditions.

[Visual 4 – symbolism in the marriage service]

There is much in the Marriage Service that is acted rather than spoken. Some of the symbolic acts are more obvious than others: the joining of hands, the couple facing each as they make vows, the exchanging of rings, for example, and the way some priests wrap a stole around the couple's hands at the proclamation of the marriage. There are customary acts, not necessarily expressions of Christian marriage as such. They include the entry of the bride into church with her father or supporter, and her exit with her husband, the putting back of the bride's veil, and the presence of a congregation.

 DISCUSSION
Wedding candles are a traditional symbol used in some Christian churches. A candle is set in the middle of the altar, and, after the couple have been declared husband and wife, a light is taken from each altar candle and handed to the bride and groom by a member of their own family. Together the couple light their own wedding candle – a symbol of two individuals, and two families, who are now joined in marriage. Do you think that extra imagery and symbolism such as this is helpful in marriage services? Can you think of (or have you experienced) other ways of enriching the service?

'BEFORE AND AFTER' THE MARRIAGE SERVICE

Marriage is not just the one ceremony, it is a way of life. In the process of marriage, people get engaged, prepare for marriage, enter into it and continue married life until one of the partners dies or the marriage ends in divorce. In general, however, the Church has perceived itself to be involved only in the actual wedding ceremony. Other rituals, such as engagements and anniversaries, have been left for private and family observation and have not been seen as matters in which the Church might be involved.

One of the strengths of the *Common Worship* material is that it offers additional prayers and services to hallow preparation for marriage and the whole of married life. Prayers are given, for example, for use when the banns are called. A service of 'Thanksgiving for Marriage' is also given which can be adapted for a number of different occasions such as a reaffirmation of vows, on an anniversary, say, or on other occasions.

There may be additional occasions in the life of a couple, where worship and prayer might be offered. The Church's official worship material does not make specific provision, say, to celebrate an engagement, but it would be possible to do so by adapting some of the prayers that are given.

 DISCUSSION
The group may like to list other events relating to marriage for which worship and prayer might be appropriate and make suggestions as to how the church might respond.

DIVORCE AND REMARRIAGE

Church ceremonies after civil marriages

In 1985 the General Synod of the Church of England authorized a Service of Prayer and Dedication after a civil marriage. The service was mainly, though not solely, used when one or both of those marrying had been previously married and the ex-partner was still living. The Service of Prayer and Dedication included prayers of penitence and reconciliation and also a promise of support from the congregation. The optional prayers included one or two for families.

From the mid-1980s many clergy have felt able to offer Christian marriage to some of those who had previously been divorced. While not officially encouraging the practice, the House of Bishops drew up guidelines in 1985 to assist discernment. In February 2000 the House of Bishops produced a discussion document on marriage in church after divorce. The paper sought to respond to an evident and increasing pastoral need: over a third of all marriages today end in divorce. While the Church continues to affirm the lifelong nature of marriage, it also wants to respond sensitively to the increasingly common requests for remarriage after divorce.

 DISCUSSION
Some Christians say that all marriages should be civil marriages, and that Christians who want a service in church could have a wedding Eucharist or an appropriate service of blessing after the civil ceremony. What do you think?

The new Marriage Act allows for marriages to take place in premises other than churches and register offices. This may decrease the number of requests for church marriages. Should we mind?

session 11 – HANDOUT

Common Worship – Pastoral Introduction to the Marriage Service

A wedding is one of life's great moments, a time of solemn commitment as well as good wishes, feasting and joy. St John tells us how Jesus shared in such an occasion at Cana, and gave there a sign of new beginnings as he turned water into wine. Marriage is intended by God to be a creative relationship, as his blessing enables husband and wife to love and support each other in good times and in bad, and to share in the care and upbringing of children. For Christians marriage is also an invitation to share life together in the spirit of Jesus Christ. It is based upon a solemn, public and lifelong covenant between a man and a woman, declared and celebrated in the presence of God and before witnesses.

On this their wedding day the bride and bridegroom face each other, make their promises and receive God's blessing. You are witnesses of the marriage, and express your support by your presence and your prayers. Your support does not end today: the couple will value continued encouragement in the days and years ahead of them.

Love is patient; love is kind; love is not envious or boastful or arrogant or rude. It does not insist on its own way; it is not irritable or resentful; it does not rejoice in wrongdoing, but rejoices in the truth. It bears all things, believes all things, hopes all things, endures all things.
1 Corinthians 13.4–7

DISCUSSION QUESTIONS

THE CAUSES FOR WHICH MATRIMONY WAS ORDAINED (*Book of Common Prayer*)
First, It was ordained for the procreation of children, to be brought up in the fear and nurture of the Lord, and to the praise of his holy Name.

Secondly, It was ordained for a remedy against sin, and to avoid fornication; that such persons as have not the gift of continency might marry, and keep themselves undefiled members of Christ's body.

Thirdly, It was ordained for the mutual society, help, and comfort, that the one ought to have of the other, both in prosperity and adversity.

DECLARATIONS (*Common Worship*)
The minister says to the congregation
Will you, the families and friends of N and N, support and uphold them in their marriage now and in the years to come?
We will.

'GIVING AWAY' (*Note 6: Common Worship Marriage Service*)
This traditional ceremony is optional. Immediately before the couple exchange vows the minister may ask: *Who brings this woman to be married to this man?*
The bride's father (or mother, or another member of her family or a friend representing the family) gives the bride's right hand to the minister who puts it in the bridegroom's right hand. Alternatively, after the bride and bridegroom have made their Declarations, the minister may ask the parents of bride and bridegroom in these or similar words: *N and N have declared their intention towards each other. As their parents, will you now entrust your son and daughter to one another as they come to be married?* Both sets of parents respond: **We will.**

OPENING WORSHIP
(Common Worship Collect for the 2nd Sunday after Trinity)

> Lord, you have taught us that all our doings without love are nothing worth: send your Holy Spirit and pour into our hearts that most excellent gift of love, the true bond of peace and of all virtues, without which whoever lives is counted dead before you. Grant this for your only Son Jesus Christ's sake. Amen.

CLOSING WORSHIP
(Common Worship prayer at the Calling of the Banns)

> Lord, the source of all true love, we pray for these couples. Grant to them joy of heart, seriousness of mind and reverence of spirit, that as they enter into the oneness of marriage they may be strengthened and guided by you, through Jesus Christ our Lord. Amen.

Before the Next Session – Funerals
What do you think are the main purposes of the funeral service?

Think about some of the funerals you have attended. What sort of things about them do you remember as being particularly helpful?

What was especially unhelpful or disappointing?

1

THE MARRIAGE SERVICE

christian worship

	Banns/licence
Preface	
	The Declarations
Collect, Readings, Sermon	
	The Vows
	Giving of Rings
	Proclamation
Blessing of Marriage	
	Registration
Prayers	
Blessing	

legal ceremony

2

WHERE CHRISTIAN MARRIAGE TAKES PLACE

groom's house	0 A.D.	
	300 A.D.	at home but 'more of a church affair'– with ordained minister
	900 A.D.	
marriage at church door; Eucharist at altar		
	1549 A.D.	marriage in nave; Eucharist at altar
	1662 A.D. B.C.P.	
marriage at chancel step; prayers at Lord's table	2000 A.D. C.W.	marriage in church – possibly in context of Holy Communion

3

HERE COMES THE BRIDE

a piece of property given away?

entrusted by their parents to each other?

the couple stand before the minister?

4

SYMBOLISM IN THE MARRIAGE SERVICE

M
a
r veil   rings
r
i rice   joining of hands
a
g confetti   wrapping stole – 'tying the knot'
e

witnesses

bridesmaids   best man

FUNERALS

PART A – GETTING STARTED

Aim

To consider the place of the funeral service and to explore some of the 'before and after the funeral' provisions in *Common Worship*.

Leader's preparation

Read through the funeral services in *Common Worship* and in *The Book of Common Prayer*.

Check whether any of the group members have recent and painful memories of bereavement. It might be helpful to talk with them before the session; this could be a difficult one for them.

Decide which prayers, songs and readings you are going to use in the times of worship, and photocopy any material you need to say together.

Opening worship

Begin by reading a Scripture passage, such as Romans 8.31–39, that sets death in the context of the resurrection. (Depending on the group, this may be an appropriate moment for members to name anyone important to them who has died recently.) Say a prayer or a litany, such as no. 67 *Pastoral Services*, p. 372; an adapted version is printed on the handout). End by saying together Romans 8.37–39. (A lit candle might be a particularly helpful focus for the worship in this session.)

Session starter

In pairs, share responses to the 'before the session' questions and discuss what makes a funeral 'good'.

In plenary, collect everyone's answers to the last question.

Look at Visual 1. Who have we focused on in our assumptions about what a funeral is and does? Have we considered all those involved: the deceased; close family; church family; the wider community?

Look at 'the words that may be read' before the *Common Worship* Funeral Service (handout). For whom might these words be especially helpful?

PART B – HEART OF THE MATTER

See pages 100–3

PART C – TAKING IT FURTHER

Final discussion

Looking back over all the services and prayers discussed in the sessions, consider how the various services can help Christians travel the journey of life. (You may like to draw a picture to illustrate your thinking.) Share your thoughts with the group. How might the *Common Worship* services be used in your church to further enrich and assist the journey of life of worshippers?

Reading and resources

The Funeral Services in *Common Worship* and *The Book of Common Prayer*.

Walter, Tony *Funerals and How to Improve Them* (Hodder and Stoughton, 1990). Very readable analysis of how our society deals with death, with excellent creative suggestions as to how our funeral liturgies can help.

Bentley, J., Best, A., Hunt, J. (eds.) *Funerals: A Guide* (Hodder and Stoughton, 1995). This is much more than a useful guide for planning funerals, it is also a spiritual resource for the bereaved, containing a wide selection of Scripture passages, prayers and other readings relating to death and resurrection.

Horton, R. Anne *Using Common Worship: Funerals* (CHP/*Praxis* 2000). A practical introduction for those who will use the *Common Worship* funeral material.

Cocksworth, Christopher *Prayer and the Departed* (Grove Worship Series no. 142) (Grove, 1997). A careful and balanced look at a controversial subject.

Davies, J. Douglas *Death, Ritual and Belief.* (Cassell, 1997). A thorough and wide-ranging study.

Closing worship

Say a Canticle, e.g., 'A Song of Faith', or 'A Song of the Redeemed' (Canticles for use at Funeral and Memorial Services in *Common Worship: Pastoral Services,* pp. 398, 399). Sing or say an Easter – or another appropriate – hymn or song, such as 'Love's redeeming work is done', 'For all the saints', or 'Guide me, O thou great redeemer'. End with the Grace, or a blessing or ending prayer such as nos 82, 83, *Pastoral Services* p. 378.

The old order has passed away, as you welcome him into paradise

PART B – HEART OF THE MATTER

[VISUAL 1 – WHO IS THE FUNERAL FOR?]

People do not attend funeral services very frequently, and mourners, of course, are reluctant worshippers. The funeral service is, however, one of the most powerful and significant of all our church services. The funerals that most people attend are nearly always of people very dear to them. They look for a service which honours the person who has died, proclaims their faith, and the faith of the dead person, supports them in grief and enables them to walk forward in hope.

The Church wants to respond to all these expectations. The funeral services both proclaim the faith of the Church in the face of death and also express the love of God for the person who has died and for those who are bereaved.

 DISCUSSION
Give group members a few moments to read the box 'Why Funerals?' on the handout. Which reasons do they think are of most importance, and for whom?

EARLY CHRISTIAN FUNERALS

There is no complete description of an early Christian funeral. All we have are clues and part references. Some light on early Christian practice comes from comparing Christian references with the funeral practices of other cultural traditions of the day. Some of these practices were absorbed into Christian funerals; others were roundly rejected.

The ancient Roman practice began with various ceremonies in the home, including the preparation of the body. The funeral procession to the graveside took place at night. Everyone wore black. And the burial or cremation was followed by a funeral feast at the graveside. After the funeral there were purification ceremonies for the relatives and also for the dead person's house.

For the Jewish people the burial of their dead was an important religious obligation. After the body had been prepared for burial it was taken in procession to the graveside. There were readings and prayers, some of these very similar to Christian texts. Among the prayers said was the *Kaddish*, a prayer for the departed that has been said by the Jews since very early times and is still used today.

There was nearly always a funeral meal at home after Jewish burials. Rites of purification followed; until these had been completed, mourners were not allowed to carry out any other religious duties. Contact with death had rendered them 'unclean'.

We find tiny clues as to early Christian funeral practice in the New Testament writings and in other written records from the first three centuries of Christianity. The gospel references to the burials of Jesus and of Lazarus (Luke 23.50 ff.) tell us something of the way Jewish people prepared the bodies of their dead for burial. In another story, that of the raising to life of the widow of Nain's son, we read of a crowd of mourners processing to the place of burial (Luke 7.11ff).

There are further references in later Christian texts, all demonstrating a strong sense of resurrection hope. Funeral ceremonies began at home. Prayers were said as the body was ceremonially washed, anointed, and wrapped in white linen. The dead person was carried in procession to the cemetery, which was always outside the city walls. As the mourners processed they sang psalms of hope and praise and there were victory shouts of 'alleluia'. Because the dead Christian was seen as sharing in Christ's victory over death, the funeral procession was a triumphal occasion, rather like the processions that accompanied victorious generals on their return home from battle. People wore white clothes, they carried palm leaves and lights, and incense was burned. Everything took place in broad daylight.

At the graveside, the community said prayers and celebrated the Eucharist. The prayers expressed a belief in the communion that continues to exist between the living and the dead. The mourners gave the kiss of peace to the corpse. Bodies were buried with the feet pointing towards the east – a sign of hope in the Second Coming. Christians spoke about death as a 'heavenly birthday'. It was something to celebrate. After the funeral everyone went back to the dead person's home to share in an agape, a fellowship meal with prayers. More services were held on various days after the death, and on its anniversary.

 DISCUSSION
What special things do we do at home before, during and after a funeral?
Are there any similarities with early Christian practices?

FROM HOPE TO FEAR

By the Middle Ages the atmosphere of Christian funerals was very different. Christians were far more fearful in their attitude to death, and this fear was reflected in the words of the funeral service. This was full of images of hell, purgatory and the terrors of dying unprepared. Graphic paintings of the Last Judgement on the walls of the parish churches reinforced people's fears of judgement. The theory behind such paintings was, perhaps, that if it was possible to scare the hell out of people it might just result in scaring them out of hell. The *Dies irae* (Day of wrath) chant, a twelfth- or thirteenth-century composition, vividly conveys the medieval Christian's attitude to death. English translations can be found in many hymn books; for example, *English Hymnal* 351, *A&M Revised* 466, *New English Hymnal* 524.

Mourners at medieval funerals wore black. In England, burials mostly took place in parish churchyards; the body was carried from the home to church in procession. It was met at the lychgate by the priest, and carried into the church as penitential psalms were said or sung. The Eucharist (Mass) was celebrated. There were various symbolic ceremonies before the interment, including the absolution of the dead person by the priest, the incensing of the body and its sprinkling with holy water.

DISCUSSION
Christian burial ceremonies have always reflected something of the tension between mourning and celebration.

Discuss how we reflect these tensions in our response to death today, e.g., the liturgical colour for funerals, the colours worn by mourners, the meal afterwards, etc.

THE ENGLISH REFORMATION

The European and English reformers challenged many of the theological perceptions of the later medieval Church. Those challenges and new understandings were reflected in the changes that Thomas Cranmer, and others, made to the services and prayers of the Church in England. The burial service, like other services, was radically revised.

One aspect of medieval Christian belief to which the reforming theologians in Europe were particularly opposed was the doctrine of purgatory. Medieval Christians believed that after death, souls moved into an 'in-between' state during which they underwent a time of painful spiritual purgation in preparation for heaven. The reformers, on the other hand, taught that the death and resurrection of Christ was sufficient for the salvation of Christian believers.

Article XXII (of the Thirty Nine Articles)

The Romish Doctrine concerning Purgatory, Pardons, Worshipping and Adoration, as well of Images as of Reliques, and also invocation of saints, is a fond thing vainly invented, and grounded upon no warranty of Scripture, but rather repugnant to the Word of God.

Although the reformers managed to set aside people's fears of purgatory, other attitudes were more difficult to dislodge. On the continent Luther wanted less mournful and more hopeful rites with 'comforting hymns of the forgiveness of sins, of rest, sleep, life, and of the resurrection of the dead'.

In England, however, revisions were more conservative. In the 1549 Prayer Book, Thomas Cranmer's service stressed hope through Christ and the resurrection. It was comprised of four elements: churchyard procession; the burial, words of committal and prayers commending the deceased to God; a short office for the dead to be said in church before or after the burial; and an optional Eucharist. In the short-lived 1552 Prayer Book, however, with its movement towards Scripture and away from 'fond things vainly invented', there was no reference at all to the Eucharist, no

singing of psalms and no prayers for the dead. The brief service took place almost entirely at the graveside. It included biblical sentences, prayers, and two New Testament readings: Revelation 14.13, 1 Corinthians 15.20–58. The priest said the words of committal while earth was cast upon the body. This was the only remaining symbolic act.

The 'final' version of the funeral service in the 1662 Book of Common Prayer was a little less austere than the order of 1552. Its mixture of comfort, challenge and penitence in the awesome presence of death served the Church of England's needs for nearly three hundred years. Mourners were comforted by the assurance of their belief in the benefits of Christ's resurrection and by the concept of death as a deliverance 'from the miseries of this sinful world'. They prayed that when they died, they might be found to be 'acceptable in thy sight'. Elements of resurrection and hope were present in the 1662 service, though not as freely or as joyfully as in the earliest Christian rites.

DISCUSSION
Have you ever attended a *Book of Common Prayer* burial service?

What particular impressions do you recall?

What do you think might have been the gains and losses of the Reformation changes?

TWENTIETH-CENTURY REVISIONS

In 1928, major revisions to *The Book of Common Prayer* were proposed. The suggested revisions for the funeral service provided for some additional readings and prayers – including a few optional prayers that mentioned the deceased by name and that some people felt able to say 'for' the dead person. (This was the first time that the Church of England funeral service had included any prayers that mentioned the dead person's name in the service.) The 1928 Book suggested changes as to the overall shape of the service, and to where different parts of it might take place, for example,

DISCUSSION
Although cremation was available in England from the beginning of the twentieth century, the Churches were slow to accept cremation as an acceptable means of disposal. This was partly due to its associations with pagan funerals and the rites of other faiths, and partly due to the traditional emphasis on 'the dead coming out of their graves' at the resurrection. Since the mid–twentieth century numbers of cremations have increased rapidly, such that cremation is now more common than burial.

Which do you think is preferable, and what are your reasons?

church or churchyard. (The prayers preceded the committal, and the first part of the service – readings and prayers – took place inside the church rather than by the graveside.)

The 1928 Book gave an order for a Funeral of a Child. It also mentioned the possibility of a Memorial Service. And yet, despite the fact that the practice of cremation was becoming popular, the 1928 Prayer Book text made no reference to it at all. The provision for holding the major part of the service inside the church building, however, was probably not unrelated to the fact that for cremations the funeral party had to leave the church and travel to the crematorium.

THE ALTERNATIVE SERVICE BOOK (1980)

The twentieth-century saw far-reaching changes in almost every aspect of life. Contemporary cultural influences also affected Christian thinking about death. Arguably, twentieth-century worshippers had neither the full-blooded hope of the early Christians nor yet the fear of their medieval predecessors. There was a reluctance to think and talk about death – even as part of the Christian message. Christian funerals were not always conducted within a church but increasingly took place, for example, in a public cemetery or in a crematorium. Cremations had become more usual than burials. English burial customs became much more functional and reflected the secular, post-Christian society which was England. Everything served to protect people as far as possible from the cold reality and threat of death. The funeral business rapidly became a professional business; funerals were smoothly run, not by the clergy, but by professional funeral directors. A religious aspect was no longer assumed.

The Alternative Service Book 1980 Funeral Service attempted to address these cultural changes in two ways. Additional texts were sensitive to new pastoral needs and fuller provision was made for the funerals of children. The practice of cremation was acknowledged; prayers at the interment of ashes were added. As if to counter an increasing secular society, however, the services deliberately celebrated the Christian hope. The texts emphasized resurrection joy and hope almost to the exclusion of grief and mourning. The possible eucharistic context for funerals was stressed. There were several new optional prayers, many for those who mourn. One or two prayers gave the opportunity to remember the departed by name. The theological content was carefully phrased and set a clear context of resurrection hope for all God's faithful people.

DISCUSSION
How important is it that funeral services (a) respond to the human need to grieve, and (b) proclaim Christian joy in the hope of resurrection?

COMMON WORSHIP

The *Common Worship* funeral services have been thoroughly reshaped to serve the members of the Church of England in the twenty-first century. Today's society is increasingly aware of people's psychological needs. The new services demonstrate this awareness in many ways, not least in the way they respond to the nature of grief and to the pastoral needs of those who mourn. Sensitive provision is made for the needs of those who are dying and the various stages of the bereavement 'journey' (Visual 2).

There are services and prayers which minister to the dying. There are prayers at the time of death, and before and after the funeral. There are sensitive and gentle resources for the funerals of children. For the first time, provision is made for a memorial service.

The services also take into account the many different needs of those who gather for a funeral service, whether in crematorium, chapel or church. In these and other ways the *Common Worship* services are well suited to contemporary needs, and, sensitively handled, should encourage more people to use the local parish church and clergy for their funeral services and pastoral care.

Ministry at the time of death

People, even many Christian people, are still very fearful of dying, if not of death. The *Common Worship* services and prayers at the time of death (Visual 3) should help Christians respond to that fear not least by the fact that using them with people is an explicit acknowledgement that they are dying, and will soon die. Yet these prayers are very much a continuation of the normal spiritual practices of daily life and, as such, support everyone – both those who are dying and those who watch and care for them.

The use of Scripture, albeit in very short phrases, makes links with peoples' memories of regularly hearing and reading the Bible. Prayers of repentance and reconciliation are a part of every Christian's daily life, though they take on added significance at the time of death. It is natural for Christians to read the Scriptures together, and to pray for each other and to break bread together in Holy Communion; family and close Christian friends are encouraged to continue to do these things together as death approaches. We are less accustomed to the laying on of hands and anointing, but the *Common Worship* services of wholeness and healing may help gradually to introduce these things into our worshipping lives (see Session 10).

DISCUSSION
If there are group members who have themselves experienced sharing in the ministry at the time of death, they might be willing to tell other group members what this meant to them.

At the time of death, before and after the funeral

One of the hardest things about watching with someone who is dying is often that one wants to pray but doesn't have the words. The *Common Worship* services include prayers to say when someone has just died, as well as prayers to say in the days between the death and the funeral.

> Into your hands, O Lord, we humbly entrust our *brother/sister N.* In this life you embraced *him/her* with your tender love, and opened to *him/her* the gate of heaven. The old order has passed away, as you welcome *him/her* into paradise, where there will be no sorrow, no weeping nor pain, but the fullness of peace and joy with your Son and the Holy Spirit for ever and ever. **Amen.**

During the latter part of the twentieth century, the Church of England has been blessed with a real flowering of lay ministry. Not only that, but lay people have increasingly shared in the leadership of worship, reading the Scriptures, leading the intercessions, etc. There are new, short *Common Worship* services and prayers for various situations before and after the funeral which can be led by lay people – whether family members, Christian friends, or authorized lay ministers.

 ### DISCUSSION

Have a look at some of the *Common Worship* services and prayers, such as 'for those unable to be present at the funeral', and 'at home after the funeral'.

Discuss ways in which your church might be able to minister to the bereaved through these services.

The *Common Worship* Funeral Service

The *Common Worship* Funeral Service is more sensitive to the pastoral context than its predecessors. A major change is that the service is now far more explicitly personal. In *The Book of Common Prayer*, the deceased was never even mentioned by name – it was always 'our dear *brother* or *sister*'. *Common Worship*, like *The Alternative Service Book (1980)*, provides for the deceased to be named in the prayers. *Common Worship* addtionally allows for a tribute or tributes to be made; indicates that the purpose of the sermon is to 'proclaim the gospel in the context of the death of this particular person', and sees thanksgiving for the life of the departed as an important part of the prayers.

There is greater sensitivity, too, to the needs of the congregation. People are welcomed to the service; family members or friends may give a tribute; they may also, with the consent of the ministers, place symbols of the deceased's life and faith on the coffin (Visual 4); the wide variety of prayers that are given acknowledge the reality of people's grief and pray for them. Particularly striking are the sensitive texts for use at children's funerals, and there are special prayers for those who have committed suicide or met a violent death.

 ### DISCUSSION

How important is it that funeral services be 'personal'?

Can they be *too* personal?

How might we make good use of the opportunities to place 'signs of life and faith' on the coffin?

Death and Resurrection

While the *Common Worship* funeral services consciously honour the memory of the dead person and address the needs of those who are bereaved, they don't shrink from a firm proclamation of the Christian hope. Even at the moment of death, the prayers direct those who pray to the new life that the deceased now enjoys and encourage them to place their hopes in God's goodness in the present and in his promises of eternal life.

The services have been carefully worded to respond to people's needs as they move through the grief process. The funeral service itself is structured to enable a gentle progression from looking backwards in grief towards looking forward in hope. The introduction to the Memorial Service reminds the congregation that 'we look not to things that are seen but to the things that are unseen; for the things that are seen are transient, but the things that are unseen are eternal'. The concluding prayers ask that 'we may trust your love to give eternal life to all who believe in him', and also encourage the worshippers to be ready to live in the light of eternity: 'The God of peace . . . make you perfect in every good work to do his will.'

session 12 – HANDOUT

Common Worship **Funeral – Pastoral Introduction**

This may be read by those present before the service begins.

God's love and power extend over all creation. Every life, including our own, is precious to God. Christians have always believed there is hope in death as in life, and that there is new life in Christ over death.

Even those who share such faith find that there is a real sense of loss at the death of a loved one. We will each have had our own experiences of their life and death, with different memories and different feelings of love, grief and respect. To acknowledge this at the beginning of the service should help us to use this occasion to express our faith and our feelings as we say farewell, acknowledge our loss and our sorrow, and to reflect on our own mortality. Those who mourn need support and consolation. Our presence here today is part of that continuing support.

OPENING WORSHIP

We pray with confidence to God our Father, who raised Christ his Son from the dead for the salvation of all, saying
Lord in your mercy
hear our prayer.
Be close to those who mourn: increase their faith in your undying love.

May we be strengthened in our faith, live the rest of our lives in following your Son, and be ready when you shall call us to eternal life.

Show your mercy to the dying: strengthen them with hope, and fill them with the peace and joy of your presence.

Lord, we commend all those who have died to your unfailing love, that in them your will may be fulfilled; and we pray that we may share with them in your eternal kingdom; through Jesus Christ our Lord. **Amen.**

CLOSING WORSHIP

Refrains for Canticles for use at Funeral and Memorial Services (*Common Worship*)
A Song of Faith
> **God raised Christ from the dead,**
> **the Lamb without spot or stain.**
A Song of the Redeemed
> **Proclaim the time of the Lord's favour,**
> **and comfort all who grieve.**

SIGNS OF LIFE AND FAITH
[VISUAL 4]

Sprinkling the coffin with water
With this water we call to mind *N*'s baptism. As Christ went through the deep waters of death for us, so may he bring us to the fullness of resurrection life.

Covering the coffin with a pall
We are already God's children, but what we shall be has not yet been revealed. Yet we know that when Christ appears we shall be like him, for we shall see him as he is.

Placing a Bible on the coffin
Lord Jesus Christ, your living and imperishable word brings us to new birth. Your eternal promises to us and to *N* are proclaimed in the Bible.

Placing a cross on the coffin
Lord Jesus Christ, for love of *N* and each one of us you bore our sins on the cross.

Why Funerals?
- the reverent disposal of a body?
- to honour the deceased person?
- help us accept the reality of the death?
- help us prepare for our own death?
- to give thanks for the life of the deceased?
- in hope of the resurrection?
- to allow us to move on to the next stage of life?
- to help with the grief process?
- an act of love?
- to set death in the context of Christian faith?

session 12 – VISUALS

1. WHO IS THE FUNERAL FOR?

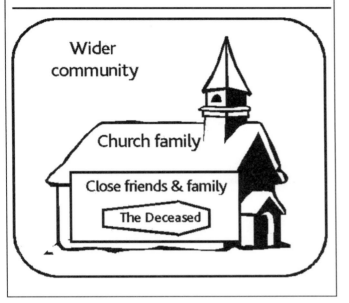

Wider community

Church family

Close friends & family

The Deceased

2. THROUGH DEATH TO LIFE

Ministry at time of death → Before the funeral → Funeral → After the funeral

Common Worship

3. HOW THE CHURCH HELPS US FACE DEATH

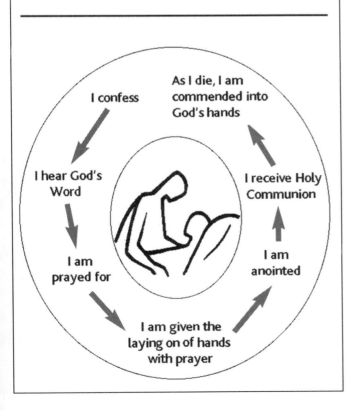

As I die, I am commended into God's hands

I confess

I hear God's Word

I am prayed for

I am given the laying on of hands with prayer

I am anointed

I receive Holy Communion

4. SIGNS OF LIFE AND FAITH

Light a candle

Place Bible on coffin

Common Worship

Place cross on coffin

Sprinkle coffin with water

Cover coffin with pall

1

THE MARRIAGE SERVICE

christian worship | | **legal ceremony**

Banns/licence

Preface

The Declarations

Collect, Readings, Sermon

The Vows

Giving of Rings

Proclamation

Blessing of Marriage

Registration

Prayers

Blessing

2

WHERE CHRISTIAN MARRIAGE TAKES PLACE

I receive Holy Communion

(4)

SIGNS OF LIFE AND FAITH

Light a candle

Place Bible on coffin

Common Worship

Place cross on coffin

Sprinkle coffin with water

Cover coffin with pall